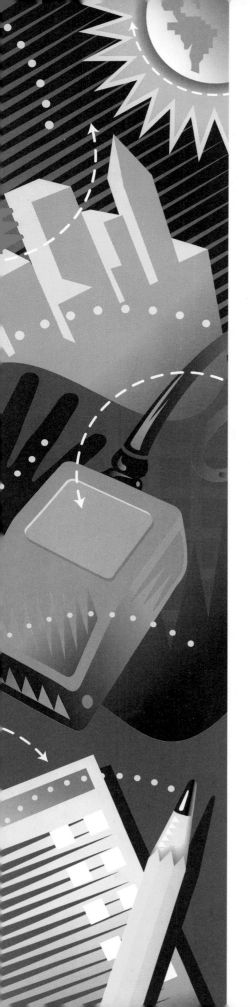

NEW VISTAS

2

STUDENT BOOK

H. DOUGLAS BROWN

ANNE ALBARELLI-SIEGFRIED
North Harris Montgomery Community College

ALICE SAVAGE
North Harris Montgomery Community College

MASOUD SHAFIEI
University of Houson

Internet Activities by Howard Beckerman
Heartworks International, Inc., Stony Brook, New York

Library of Congress Cataloging–in–Publication Data

Brown, H. Douglas, 1941–
    New vistas, Student book 2 / H. Douglas Brown.
         p.   cm.
    ISBN 0–13–908237–9
    1. English language– – Textbooks for foreign speakers.   I. Title.
PE1128.B7248   1999
428.2′4--dc21
                                   98-14842
                                   CIP

Publisher: *Mary Jane Peluso*
Series Editor: *Stella Reilly*
Main Development Editor: *Kathleen Ossip*
In-house Development Editors: *Janet Johnston, Andrea Bryant*
Editorial Assistant: *Alison Kinney*
Director of Production
  and Manufacturing: *Aliza Greenblatt*
Production/Design Manager-Multimedia: *Paul Belfanti*
Electronic Production Editor: *Carey Davies*
Manufacturing Manager: *Ray Keating*
Art Director: *Merle Krumper*
Cover Coordinator: *Merle Krumper, Eric Dawson*
Illustrators: *Carlotta Tormey, Matthew Daniel, Betsy Day, Andrew Lange, Shelly Matheis,*
  Gabriel Polonsky, Len Schalansky, Catherine Doyle Sullivan
Realia: *Carey Davies, Eric Dawson, Steven Greydanus, Michelle LoGerfo, Wendy Wolf*
Interior Design: *Eric Dawson*
Cover Design: *Carmine Vecchio*

10 9 8 7 6 5 4 3

ISBN 0-13-908237-9

Reviewers: Peggy Armstrong, *Kaplan Educational Services;* Leslie Biaggi, *Miami-Dade Community College;* Ulysses D'Aquila, *City College of San Francisco;* M. Sadiq Durrani, *BNC Santa Cruz;* Kathy Hamilton, *Elk Grove Adult Education;* Peter Jarvis, *New York City Board of Education Adult Division;* Kevin Keating, *University of Arizona;* Margaret Masterson, *Bethune Middle School;* Joanne Mooney, *University of Pennsylvania;* Janet K. Orr, *Shanghai Centre, Beijing;* Cheryl Pearson, *University of Houston;* Randy Schafer, *Free-lance Instructor, Japan;* Tammy Smith-Firestone, *Edgewood Language Institute;* Maria Rita Vieira, *Yazigi Language Schools, Brasil*

Contents

Grammmar and Pronunciation	Communication Skills	
	LISTENING AND SPEAKING	READING AND WRITING
• Simple present *vs.* present continuous; affirmative and negative tag questions and short responses: *do/does,* and *is/are* • Tag questions	Make introductions; ask for personal information; talk about everyday activities; talk about appropriate classroom behavior; confirm a statement; engage in small talk; discuss traditions and customs	Read for specific information; set up a personal journal
• Simple past: regular/irregular verbs; affirmative and negative statements; *yes/no, Wh-,* past tag questions and responses •Irregular verbs: The present and past forms	Sequence events; ask about the past; compare the past and present; describe personal life events; ask for confirmation; discuss historical events and achievements	Write a paragraph; make a time line; read a short magazine article; write a simple autobiography; revise written material
• Modals: *can, could, may, might, should* and their negatives; past continuous: affirmative statements and *yes/no* questions and responses • Reduced syllables	Talk about possibility; invite someone by phone; accept and decline an invitation orally; leave and take a telephone message; talk about ongoing past activities; talk about the right thing to do in social situations	Write a message from an answering machine; write predictions; write an invitation and a response to an invitation; read a newspaper article
• Modals: *have to, had to, must* and their negatives, *may* (permission); object pronouns; future with *going to* • Minimal pairs: [b] [p]	Make excuses; compare classroom behavior in different cultures; discuss school policies; talk about personal and academic goals; make future predictions; discuss learning styles	Read about school policies; write about goals; complete a learning style questionnaire; identify personality types; describe yourself in writing
• Comparative adjectives: regular and irregular; *used to*: affirmative and negative statements and *yes/no* questions and short responses • Minimal pairs: [b] [v]	Talk about places in a neighborhood; ask for and give directions; compare two places in a town or city; talk about holidays; talk about past habits and customs; describe differences between two cities	Write a paragraph; read for specific information; write a journal entry about goals
• Imperatives: affirmative and negative; verbs followed by infinitives • Statement or Question?	Talk about health problems and remedies; make suggestions; make a doctor's appointment; give advice; discuss a healthy diet; talk about preferences, likes, and dislikes in food; listen to advice about a healthy diet	Take notes; read about alternative medicine; write a short report; read and answer letters asking for advice; write about an illness or accident
• Compound sentences: *and, or, but, so*; superlative adjectives: regular and irregular; comparisons with *as . . . as* • Minimal pairs: [b] [d]	Talk about purchases; exchange a purchase; compare features of stores and items; make a catalog purchase; give reasons for returning a purchase; role play business transactions; listen to television ads	Write a letter of complaint; analyze an ad; write an ad for a school; write about fashion, television ads, desirable products, and comparing stores
• Present perfect: statements with *already, yet*, with *have/has* questions and responses; *too/either*; contractions • Full forms and contractions with *have*	Talk about budgets; talk about past actions; open a checking account; call an account information line; listen to a radio broadcast for specific details; listen to information about budgets	Record information in a check register; compare and make budgets; write about learning English, credit cards, and saving money, make a "to do" list
• Complex sentences with *before, after, when, because* • Minimal pairs: [θ] thank / [t] tank	Ask for a letter of recommendation; discuss desirable jobs; call about an advertised job; listen for information about a job and a job interview; role play an interview	Write a letter of recommendation; read and write employment ads; write about skills and abilities; read about careers
• Simple future: *will; will* with *yes/no* questions and responses; real conditional: *if*-clauses; possessive pronouns • Contractions with *will*	Talk about predictions; make promises; talk about future goals and possibilities; share memories; predict future events; talk about superstitions	Write about predictions, superstitions, and goals

To the Teacher

New Vistas is a series that features the best of what has come to be known as "communicative language teaching," including recent developments in creating interactive, learner-centered curriculum. With **New Vistas,** your students become actively involved in their own language acquisition through collaboration with you as their guide and facilitator.

The Components of *New Vistas*

Student Books

The five-level student books begin with *Getting Started.* Here, students learn basic life skills and vocabulary. Then, in the subsequent levels, students develop their competence and proficiency step by step in all four skills.

Primary features of all the *Student Books* include a storyline with multi-ethnic characters, providing students with opportunities to be personally involved in real-life contexts for learning; a carefully graded series of pronunciation modules; many opportunities for group and pair interaction; listening comprehension exercises; a new and exciting online feature that introduces students to Internet technology; a strategy-awareness section in each unit that stimulates students to reflect on their own preferred pathways to success; and end-of-unit grammar and communication skills summaries.

Teacher's Resource Manuals

For each unit, the *Teacher's Resource Manual* provides an overview of topics, functions, communication skills, and skills standards covered. This is followed by step-by-step, explicit teaching instructions; answer keys for the exercises in the *Student Books* and the *Workbooks*, tapescripts for the listening and pronunciation exercises; grammar activity masters; and placement and achievement tests.

Workbooks

These supplements provide numerous written exercises that reinforce the grammar points and structures taught in the *Student Books*. *Workbook* exercises are suitable for additional in-class practice or for homework.

The Audio Programs

The audiotapes provide stimulating listening and pronunciation practice that add to the authenticity of classroom pedagogy.

Lesson 1

In this lesson, you will

- make formal and informal introductions.
- ask a new acquaintance about himself or herself.
- describe actions in progress.
- talk about appropriate classroom behavior.

I'm studying in California.

Look at the picture. Then listen as you read the conversation.

Nelson: We're having great weather, aren't we?

Pablo: We sure are. By the way, I'm Pablo Bonilla.

Nelson: Hello. I'm Nelson. Nelson Balewa.

Pablo: What do you do, Nelson?

Nelson: I'm a student. I'm studying in California.

Pablo: Really? Am I glad to meet you! I'm looking for a school in California.

Nelson: Why don't you try our school? My friends and I can help you apply.

Pablo: That would be great!

Nelson: My friend Oscar is over there surfing. He's from Spain. And Ivan is from Russia. He's playing volleyball with Oscar's uncle. Come on, I'll introduce you.

Nelson: Mr. Garcia, Ivan. I'd like you to meet Pablo Bonilla.

Mr. Garcia: It's a pleasure to meet you, Pablo.

Pablo: How do you do, Mr. Garcia?

Ivan: Hi, Pablo.

Pablo: Hi.

Nelson: Pablo is planning to study in the United States. He has questions about our school.

Ivan: We'll be happy to help you, Pablo. You can also call Mrs. Brennan, our teacher.

Pablo: Thanks. I'll do that!

Pair **Ask your partner:** _How did you find out about our school?_

1 I'd like you to meet . . .

🔊 Listen to the conversations. Which introduction is more formal? Which is informal? Why do you think one is formal, the other informal?

Ivan: Hey, Gina! This is Pablo. He's a new student.

Gina: Hi, Pablo.

Pablo: Hi. Nice to meet you. What's your name again?

Gina: It's really Regina, but everybody calls me Gina.

Ivan: Mrs. Brennan, I'd like you to meet Pablo Bonilla. He's a new student. Pablo, this is Mrs. Brennan, our English teacher.

Mrs. Brennan: Oh, yes. How do you do, Pablo?

Pablo: Fine, thank you. It's a pleasure to meet you, Mrs. Brennan.

Mixer Work with a partner. Walk around the room. Introduce your partner to other students. Practice both formal and informal introductions.

2 Everybody calls me . . .

Pair Practice these questions with your teacher. Then ask your partner.

1. What's your first name?

2. Does your name have a special meaning? Why did your parents choose this name?

3. Do you like your name?

4. Do you have a nickname?

5. What name do you want to be called?

6. What is your favorite name? Why?

7. What is the most popular name in your country?

Did you know that . . . ?
In the United States, it is correct to shake hands firmly and to look at the person when you are introduced.

Tell the class about your partner.

3 Getting to know you.

Listen to the following conversation. Then practice it with a partner.

A: What do you do?

B: I work as an assistant in an advertising agency.

A: Where do you work?

B: Right now I'm working at Ace Advertising.

A: Really? My sister works there.

B: Oh? What's her name?

Group Work in groups of four. Write a nametag for yourself and introduce yourself to the other members of your group.

Pair Talk to a member of your group. Ask these questions. Then ask some questions of your own.

1. Where are you from?

2. Where do you work?

3. Where do you live?

4. What do you do in your free time?

5. Why did you decide to come to this school?

6. Why do you want to learn English?

Tell the class about your partner. Introduce him or her to a student in a different group.

4 What are they doing?

1. sleeping
2. talking
3. taking notes
4. raising his hand
5. listening closely
6. yawning

pad   bad
pat   bat

Pair What are the students doing? Write sentences telling what each is doing.

1. _____
2. _____
3. _____
4. _____
5. _____
6. _____

Group Decide which actions are appropriate classroom behavior and which are not. Discuss your answers with the class.

5 Are you looking for a new place to live?

<u>Group</u>   Divide the class into two groups. Complete the chart with the names of members of your group.

Which student or students . . .	Names
1. is/are looking for a new place to live.	1.
2. is/are living alone.	2.
3. is/are working full time.	3.
4. is/are planning to take a trip.	4.

<u>Class</u>   Compare your answers with those of the other group and complete the sentences.

1.   _____ student(s) is/are looking for a new place to live.

2.   _____ student(s) is/are living alone.

3.   _____ student(s) is/are working full time.

4.   _____ student(s) is/are planning to take a trip.

6 Oscar is swimming.

<u>Pair</u>   Look at the two pictures. There are at least five differences between Picture A and Picture B. Can you find them? Mark each difference with an ✗.

Example:

Oscar and a man are swimming in A, but Oscar and two women are swimming in B.

A   B

In your notebook, write sentences comparing the two pictures.

Lesson 2

In this lesson, you will

- use appropriate forms of address in formal situations.
- ask for confirmation.
- confirm a statement.
- engage in small talk.

Do you have anything to declare?

The friends have a problem with the piñata. Listen to the conversation.

Nelson: I'm glad you're coming back with us, Pablo. You're going to like our school.

Pablo: I can't wait to get there.

Oscar: We're almost at the border, aren't we?

Ivan: Yes, we are, so you better put on your biggest smiles for the customs officer.

Nelson: Ah, good afternoon, sir. Nice day, isn't it?

Officer: Passports, please. How long were you in Mexico?

Nelson: A week.

Officer: Do you have anything to declare?

Nelson: Excuse me?

Officer: You're not bringing any fresh fruit or vegetables into the country, are you?

Nelson: Not exactly.

Officer: You're not joking with me, are you, young man?

Nelson: Oh, no, sir. You see, we have this piñata and . . .

Officer: Oh, I see. There's fruit in it, isn't there?

Nelson: Well . . . yes, I guess so.

Officer: Well, you're going to have to do something about that, aren't you?

Nelson: Yes, sir.

Pair With your partner, discuss what you would do about the problem with the piñata.

1 Word Bag: Forms of Address

Pair   Decide which titles are used for men, which are for women, and which are for both men and women. Write them in the correct column. Add other titles you know.

1. Ms. or Mrs.
2. Mr.
3. Judge
4. Officer
5. Professor
6. Dr.

Men	Women	Both

2 Cultural Connection

Pair   Look at some ways people greet each other. Write the word or phrase under each picture.

1. _____
2. _____
3. _____
4. _____

Group   In groups of four, talk about which greetings are used in your country. Which ones are used in formal situations?

3 Hear it. Say it.

Listen and repeat.

Tag Questions

1. A: It's a nice day, **isn't** it?
   B: Yes, it is.

2. A: You're coming at seven, **aren't** you?
   B: Yes, I am.

3. A: She **can** do it, **can't** she?
   B: Yes, she can.

4. A: You **don't** study here, **do** you?
   B: No, I don't.

5. A: He **doesn't** live here, **does** he?
   B: No, he doesn't.

6. A: We're **not** having a test, **are** we?
   B: No, we aren't.

Pair   Work with a partner. Take turns asking and answering the questions.

4 You have something to declare, don't you?

Pair   The customs officer is checking Pablo's luggage. Add tag questions to each statement. Your partner will agree with you.

1. A: It's a nice day today, _____isn't it?_____
   B: _____Yes, it is._____

2. A: You don't have anything to declare, _____
   B: _____

3. A: You aren't bringing any fruit home, _____
   B: _____

4. A: You are from the United States, _____
   B: _____

5. A: You can speak English, _____
   B: _____

6. A: You have all your suitcases, _____
   B: _____

5 The food is good, isn't it?

Pair   You are at a party. Add tag questions to the sentences to start a conversation. Your partner will agree. Then choose one and continue that conversation for as long as you can.

1. The salad is delicious, _____?

2. There aren't a lot of people here, _____?

3. You're Pablo's friend, _____?

4. It isn't a big house, _____?

5. You live near here, _____?

6. You don't live here, _____?

7. The weather isn't very good, _____?

8. You work with Ivan, _____?

6 Communication Activity, pages 121 and 122.

Class   Turn to pages 121 and 122 and follow your teacher's instructions.

Lesson 3

In this lesson, you will
- read for specific information.
- talk about everyday and ongoing activities.
- talk about traditions and customs.

From One Culture to Another

Many of our traditions and customs originated in another culture. Read the following article about one such tradition.

The Riverside News

Origins of the Piñata

The origins of the piñata are uncertain. Some experts believe that Marco Polo brought the piñata to Italy from Asia in the 12th century. The Chinese decorated cow or buffalo figures and covered them with paper. They then filled the figures with various types of seeds.

The tradition of breaking the piñata originated in Europe. In 16th-century Spain, hosts filled breakable pots with precious jewels and valuable jewelry. The guests were blindfolded and broke the pot to gather the treasures.

The game is now played in Mexico exactly the same way. However, piñatas are filled with candy and fruit instead of valuable rewards. Piñatas come in the form of stars, animals, fruits, and flowers. Some piñatas are used as practical jokes and filled with confetti or even flour.

Today piñatas can be found at parties in the United States. They represent part of a rich cultural heritage that the United States has received from cultures all over the world.

Read each statement and write the name of the country next to it.

COUNTRY

1. They filled the piñata with jewels and valuable adornments. _____

2. They decorated cow or buffalo figures and covered them with paper. _____

3. They fill the piñata with confetti or flour. _____

4. They filled the piñata with various types of seeds. _____

5. They fill the piñata with candy and fruit. _____

Class   Are there any traditions or customs in your country that come from another country? Discuss them with the class.

1 What did you do with the fruit?

🔊 Mrs. Brennan's students are having a party to start the new semester. They're breaking the piñata that Oscar, Nelson, Ivan, and Pablo brought back from Mexico. Listen to the conversation. Then listen to the questions and check (✓) the correct answers.

1. [ ] In Mazatlan.   [ ] In Mexico City.

2. [ ] Yes, he did.   [ ] No, he didn't.

3. [ ] He declared it in Customs.   [ ] He took out the fruit.

4. [ ] Pablo ate it.   [ ] Oscar ate it.

5. [ ] He ate too much fruit and got sick.   [ ] He broke the piñata.

Why does Oscar say, "I sure do"?

2 The day after the party

Pair What are the students doing right now? What do they usually do? Talk about these pictures, using the correct forms of the verbs.

Example:

Oscar usually **gets up** at 7 o'clock,
but he**'s getting up** at 8 o'clock today.

1. get up

3. have lunch/cafeteria

2. go to school/car

4. correct papers/evening

In your notebook, write sentences describing the pictures.

3 Online

 Log onto **http://www.prenhall.com/brown_activities**
The Web: Travel tips
Grammar: What's your grammar IQ?
E-mail: Making new friends

4 Wrap Up

People who are new to a country often have difficulties in the new culture. Some of these difficulties are listed in the chart. Check (✓) how difficult each one is or would be for you.

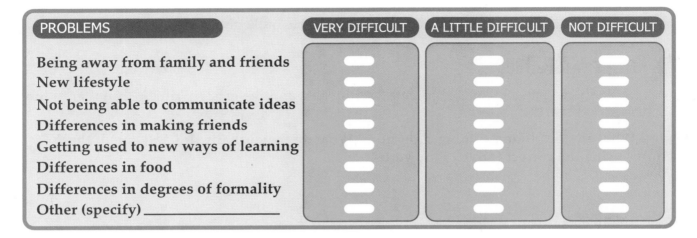

PROBLEMS	VERY DIFFICULT	A LITTLE DIFFICULT	NOT DIFFICULT
Being away from family and friends			
New lifestyle			
Not being able to communicate ideas			
Differences in making friends			
Getting used to new ways of learning			
Differences in food			
Differences in degrees of formality			
Other (specify) _____			

Pair Look at your partner's chart. Ask tag questions based on his or her answers.

Example:

Being away from family and friends is a little difficult for you, isn't it?

Group Discuss your answers in groups of four. Rank the difficulties in order of importance. (1 is the most important; 8 is the least.) Share your list with the rest of the class.

Strategies for Success

➤ **Practicing with a partner**
➤ **Reviewing tag questions**
➤ **Setting personal goals**

1. With a new partner, practice making introductions and "small talk." Talk about occupations and the difficulties of living in a new culture.

2. Continuing with that partner, use as many tag questions as possible (for example, "You live on Franklin Street, don't you?" "You don't smoke, do you?").

3. Set up your journal for the course. In your first entry, write down at least five major goals that you will try to achieve during this course, such as "I will practice using the new vocabulary words from each unit in this book," "I will write in my journal at least once a week."

CHECKPOINT

How much have you learned in this unit? Review the goals for each lesson. What skills can you confidently use now? What skills do you need to practice? List these below.

Skills I've Learned Well

_____

_____

_____

_____

Skills I Need to Practice

_____

_____

_____

_____

Learning Preferences

In this unit, which type of activity did you like the best and the least? Write the number in the box: 1 = best; 2 = next best; 3 = next; 4 = least.

- ☐ Working by myself
- ☐ Working with a partner
- ☐ Working with a group
- ☐ Working as a whole class

In this unit, which exercises helped you to learn to:

listen more effectively?   Exercise _____   read more easily?   Exercise _____

speak more fluently?   Exercise _____   write more clearly?   Exercise _____

Which exercise did you like the most? _____   Why? _____

Which exercise did you like the least? _____   Why? _____

VOCABULARY

Verbs
apply
bow
break
bring back
build
choose
come back
declare
fill
find out
hug
kiss (on the cheeks)
laugh
learn

meet
plan
shake hands
spend
start
surf
wave
whisper
yawn

Adjectives
formal
informal
popular
special

Forms of Address
Dr.
Judge
Ms.
Mrs.
Mr.
Officer
Professor

Expressions
all over
any time
as a matter of fact
come on
I can't wait
I guess so
named after
not exactly

Nouns
border
culture
hole
nickname
passport
piñata
sandcastle
semester

► GRAMMAR SUMMARY

Simple Present Tense (Review)
I **study** in the library every day.
Oscar **is** from Spain.

Present Continuous Tense (Review)
He**'s playing** volleyball.
Nelson and Oscar **are swimming**.

Present Tense: Tag Questions

Affirmative Statements	Negative Tags
You**'re** a student,	**aren't** you?
Pablo **is** Mexican,	**isn't** he?
You **like** fruit,	**don't** you?
She **speaks** Chinese,	**doesn't** she?

Short Responses
Yes, I am. *or* No, I'm not.
Yes, he is. *or* No, he isn't.
Yes, I do. *or* No, I don't.
Yes, she does. *or* No, she doesn't.

Negative Statements	Affirmative Tags
You **aren't** from the United States,	**are** you?
Gina **can't** come to the party,	**can** she?
They **aren't studying** English,	**are** they?
You **don't have** anything to declare,	**do** you?

Short Responses
No, I'm not. *or* Yes, I am.
No, she can't. *or* Yes, she can.
No, they aren't. *or* Yes, they are.
No, I don't. *or* Yes, I do.

► COMMUNICATION SUMMARY

Asking for personal information
What's your name?
Where are you from?
What do you do?

Formal introductions
Mrs. Brennan, I'd like you to meet Pablo Bonilla.
Pablo, this is Mrs. Brennan, our English teacher.
How do you do?
   Fine, thank you.
   It's a pleasure to meet you.

Talking about ongoing and everyday activities
I'm studying English in the United States.
I usually exercise every day.

Greetings
Hello, my name's Pablo Bonilla.
   Nice to meet you.

Making statements and asking for confirmation
It's a nice day, isn't it?
You aren't a student here, are you?

Lesson 1

In this lesson, you will

- sequence events in chronological order.
- ask someone about the past.
- talk about past experiences.
- compare the past with the present.

You changed, didn't you?

Look at the picture and listen to the conversation.

Yon Mi: Mrs. Brennan, yesterday I received a letter from my boyfriend in Korea.

Mrs. Brennan: What did he say?

Yon Mi: He asked me to come home. He said he missed me. He also reminded me of the things we did together last year.

Mrs. Brennan: Oh, what did you do? Did you spend a lot of time together?

Yon Mi: We explored the city and planned our future. He's lonely, Mrs. Brennan. He wants to get married soon.

Mrs. Brennan: Do you want to do that?

Yon Mi: I don't know. I wanted to marry him last year, but he wasn't ready. We decided to wait. Then I came to the United States, and now everything is different.

Mrs. Brennan: You changed, didn't you?

Yon Mi: Maybe I did. Two years ago, I wanted to get married more than anything, but now I'm not sure.

Pair What does Yon Mi have to decide? What do you think she should do? Discuss with your partner.

1 What happened?

What happened in Yon Mi's past? Number the sentences in the correct order.

_____ Yon Mi decided to come to the United States to study.

_____ Yon Mi wanted to get married.

_____ Yon Mi's boyfriend wrote Yon Mi a letter saying he was now ready to get married.

_____ Yon Mi's boyfriend said he didn't want to get married right away.

_____ Yon Mi changed her mind about getting married.

In your notebook, write a paragraph telling the story in a logical time order. Use the following words: _First, Then, Next, Finally._ **Begin your paragraph with** _"Poor Yon Mi. She can't decide what to do."_

2 Please come home soon.

Pair **Complete Han's letter. Use the correct forms of the past tense.**

Examples:

Every night we **talk** on the phone for hours.
They **eat** lunch together **every day**.
I hurry home after work **every day**.

Last night we **talked** on the phone for hours.
They **ate** lunch together **yesterday**.
I **hurried** home **two days ago**.

November 10, _____

Dear Yon Mi,
 Do you remember the happy things we did together last year? We often (eat) _ate_ lunch together at that little cafe you (like) _liked_ so much. One evening, we (have) _____ a serious talk on the phone. You (tell) _____ me how much you loved me and how you wanted to get married. We (talk) _____ for hours on the phone. Remember the day we (sing) _____ at that little karaoke club? I (be) _____ so proud of your

beautiful voice. I really miss those days when we (study) _____ in the library. You (worry) _____ about not passing your final exams, and you were very happy when you (get) _____ perfect grades! Most of all, Yon Mi, I remember the long, hot summer days when we (ride) _____ our bicycles all over the city. I (fall) _____ in love with you on those days! Please come home soon.
    Love,
    Han

3 Han fell in love with Yon Mi.

__Pair__   Ask and answer questions based on Han's letter.

Example:

A: **Did** they **eat** dinner together?

B: **No**, they **didn't**, but they **ate** lunch together.

1.   Yon Mi/love the disco
2.   they/talk about getting married
3.   Han/be proud of Yon Mi's dancing
4.   they/study at Han's house
5.   Yon Mi/cry when she got perfect grades
6.   they/ride bicycles in the city

Take turns asking and answering questions about your summer vacation or trip. Use the following ideas and add some of your own.

| How/get there | Who/go with | When/leave | How long/stay |
| What/do | Like/food | Go/sightseeing | Buy/souvenirs |

Example:

A: **Where** did you go last summer?   B: I **went** to the Niagara Falls.

4 Many years ago, there were farms here.

__Group__   Work in groups of three. Look at these pictures. Yon Mi's parents lived on a farm many years ago. Write sentences comparing the pictures. Follow the example.

many years ago/farm   today/factories

Example:

Many years ago, there were farms here. Today, there are factories.

1.   little dirt roads/highways
2.   fields/parking lots
3.   farming equipment/trucks
4.   a few people/hundreds of people
5.   trees and flowers/smog and noise
6.   animals/cars

In your notebook, write two paragraphs about the pictures. Start the first one with "Many years ago" and the second with "Today."

5 Hear it. Say it.

🔊 Listen to the verbs. Check (✓) the verb you hear.

Irregular Verbs: The Present and Past Forms

1. ( ) eat   ( ) ate   5. ( ) meet   ( ) met
2. ( ) find   ( ) found   6. ( ) know   ( ) knew
3. ( ) write   ( ) wrote   7. ( ) take   ( ) took
4. ( ) drink   ( ) drank   8. ( ) ride   ( ) rode

Pair   With a partner, practice pronouncing the present and past forms of the verbs above.

6 I got your letter.

🔊 Listen to the message that Yon Mi left on her cousin's answering machine. Write *T (true)* in the blank if the information is true, *F (false)* if the information is not true.

1. _____ Han called Yon Mi.   5. _____ Han wanted Yon Mi to go back to Korea.
2. _____ Yon Mi is not eating well.   6. _____ Yon Mi is not sleeping well.
3. _____ Yon Mi has a new boyfriend.   7. _____ Yon Mi has a new friend.
4. _____ Yon Mi passed the test.   8. _____ Yon Mi decided to study hotel management.

7 When I was a child . . .

Pair   Work with a partner. Ask each other questions about what you did when you were a child. Below are possible questions to ask. You may add more questions of your own.

1. Did you play outdoors a lot?
2. Did you ride a bike?
3. Did you visit your friends?
4. Did you like school?
5. Did you have a pet?
6. Did you get in trouble a lot?
7. Did you have fun when you were a child?

Did you know that . . . ?
In the United States, communities offer a wide variety of sports, recreational activities, and crafts after school. During summer vacations, children and teenagers can attend day camps and overnight camps.

Write a paragraph in your notebook about your childhood. Start with *When I was a child . . .* Use the questions above to help you. Add more information to make your paragraph more interesting.

Lesson 2

In this lesson, you will
- describe major personal life events.
- ask for confirmation about past events.
- describe historical events.

Do you remember . . . ?

Look at the picture and listen to the conversation.

Ann: Do you remember when we met in Berlin?

Jim: 1988. How could I forget it? Why?

Ann: I thought about it today. The Berlin Wall came down, Germany reunited, the Cold War ended. I remember all the excitement.

Jim: Yes, that was a memorable year.

Ann: We had a problem, remember? I had a job in Berlin, and you left for the Middle East. I thought I'd never see you again.

Jim: I had to leave. I came back though, didn't I?

Ann: Yes, you did, and we worked things out. My student has a similar problem. She told me her boyfriend wrote and said he misses her.

Jim: Does he want her to go back home?

Ann: Yes, he does. She still loves him, but she wants to finish the school year here. We were in the same situation, weren't we? I wanted to marry you, too, but I also wanted to stay in Germany.

Jim: I respected your decision, Ann. You're a strong woman. That's why I fell in love with you.

Ann: Gee, I hope that Yon Mi's boyfriend is as understanding as you were.

Pair Tell your partner about an important event or decision that changed your life.

1 Word Bag: Milestones

Number the pictures from 1 through 8 to show the order of events in this woman's life. Give her a name and write about her life, using the past tense. Add any information you wish.

get engaged   retire   go to school   get a job

get married   be born   graduate / college   be a parent

2 She wasn't born here, was she?

Pair   Ask and answer questions about your descriptions in Exercise 1. Use past tag questions.

Examples:

She **wasn't** born here, **was she**?	Yes, she was.	*or*	No, she wasn't.
She **didn't** graduate last year, **did she**?	Yes, she did.	*or*	No, she didn't.
They **were** born in Singapore, **weren't they**?	Yes, they were.	*or*	No, they weren't.
They **retired** early, **didn't they**?	Yes, they did.	*or*	No, they didn't.

3 Your parents got married young, didn't they?

Pair   Make guesses about events in the lives of your partner's family. Your partner will confirm or correct your guesses.

Examples:

Your mother was born in a large city, wasn't she?	Yes, she was.
Your parents got married young, didn't they?	No, they didn't. They got married when they were 30.

Report to the class about your partner's family.

4 Historical Highlights

What are five important events in the history of your country, city, or town? When did they happen? Record the events on the TIME LINE. (Example: Columbus's arrival in America.)

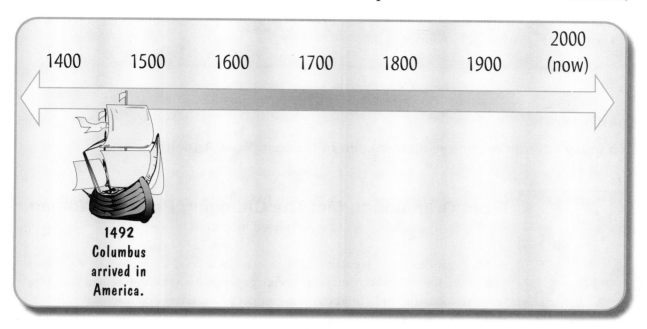

Group Work in groups of three. Write the names of two classmates in columns A and B. Ask them about the events on their time lines. Use the questions on the left. Write your classmates' answers in the boxes under their names.

Questions	A.	B.
1. What was the event?		
2. What happened?		
3. When did it happen?		
4. Where did it happen?		
5. Why was it important for your country, city, or town?		

In your notebook, write a paragraph about the history of your country, city, or town. Use the events on your time line.

5 Information Gap Activity, pages 123 and 124.

Pair Turn to pages 123 and 124 and follow your teacher's instructions.

In this lesson, you will
- read a short magazine article.
- discuss historical achievements.
- write a simple autobiography.

Women's Work

Women today have more choices than women in the past. Read Annette's story.

From Grandma to Me: The Changing Roles of Women
by Annette Dobbins

My grandmother went to college in the 1920s, but most women then did not. In fact, many women did not even have jobs. Some women worked as teachers or secretaries, but very few thought of their jobs as "careers." Some exceptions were the airplane pilot Amelia Earhart and the physician and teacher Maria Montessori.

When my mother grew up, a few things had changed. More women went to college. Some of them got professional jobs, but many of them were still pursuing the "Mrs." degree. In other words, they were in college to find a husband. After marriage, most women stayed at home and took care of their children. However, many of these women became bored. Many housekeeping jobs, such as washing dishes and clothes, became much easier and took less time with new technology. As a result, women started looking for jobs.

My mother is a good example. She went back to college when I was in high school, and now she works as a marriage counselor.

My generation of women is very different. We are serious about our education and our careers. Best of all, we have more options. We can choose what we want to be. Some of us want to be like Amelia Earhart and Maria Montessori and become leaders in our field. Others want both a family and a career. Our husbands support our decisions. They share the housework with us. Because of these choices, it is a good time to be a woman. In fact, just the other day my grandmother told me that I'm lucky. I have a great husband, who helps me with the housework. She was going to her sailing lesson!

Pair   **Discuss these questions with a partner. Then share your ideas with the class.**

1. What was a woman's life like when Annette's grandmother was young?

2. What is a "Mrs." degree? What does it mean?

3. What kinds of choices do women have today?

4. Have men's roles changed, too? How?

5. What do you think about the saying "A woman's place is in the home"?

1 Who discovered radium?

🎧 **Listen to the conversation between Pablo and Nelson. Then see how well you listened.**

1. Marie Curie discovered radium in ____.
   a. 1942
   b. 1903
   c. 1812

2. Alexander Graham Bell made the first telephone call in ____.
   a. 1876
   b. 1886
   c. 1776

3. ____ invented the light bulb.
   a. Thomas Edison
   b. Albert Einstein
   c. Jean Sibelius

4. Ts'ai Lun invented paper in ____.
   a. 1005
   b. 150
   c. 105

5. Valentina Tereshkova was ____.
   a. an astronaut
   b. a scientist
   c. an opera singer

6. Haile Selassie was ____.
   a. an inventor
   b. an emperor
   c. a race car driver

7. Ayerton Senna was a race car driver from ____.
   a. Brazil
   b. Malaysia
   c. Argentina

8. Emiliano Zapata was ____.
   a. Cuban
   b. Peruvian
   c. Mexican

Group Ask each other questions about famous people and events.

Examples:

Who **invented** the light bulb?   What **did** Thomas Edison **invent**?

2 Did you see any little green men on Mars?

Pair You're a newspaper reporter. You are going to interview your partner, who is one of these famous people:

1. an astronaut who returned from Mars
2. an explorer who discovered an island
3. a scientist who invented a cure for AIDS
4. your own idea

Choose one. With your partner, write questions a reporter might ask this person. Begin your questions with the following:

Did/Do	Where did	Why did	How long did
Is/Are/Was/Were	When did	What did	Who

Work together to answer these questions. Present your interview to the class.

Choose a famous person you admire. Go to the library or do research on the Internet to get information about this person. In your notebook, write a paragraph about this person. Use his or her name as the title.

3 Online

Log onto **http://www.prenhall.com/brown_activities**
The Web: This day in history
Grammar: What's your grammar IQ?
E-mail: Childhood memories

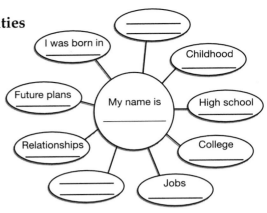

4 Wrap Up

Think about the major events in your life. In your notebook, draw an enlarged version of this chart. Use the categories listed, and add some of your own. Complete the chart with as much information as you can.

Write your autobiography, using the information in your chart.

Pair   Read your partner's autobiography and answer these questions.

1.   Which parts of the autobiography are the most interesting?

2.   Which parts do you have questions about? Do you need more information to help you understand some parts?

3.   Did your partner use the past tense correctly? Did your partner use time expressions to order his or her autobiography?

Use the answers to these questions to suggest changes to your autobiography. Then read your autobiography to the class. Do they have any suggestions or questions?

Strategies for Success

➤ **Revising writing**
➤ **Reading aloud**
➤ **Lowering anxiety**

1. In Exercise 4 of Lesson 3, you wrote your autobiography. Now, revise your writing: correct any grammatical mistakes, change words if necessary, and check spelling and punctuation.

2. Read your revised autobiography to a partner. Try to use correct pronunciation, stress, and intonation. Make any final corrections or changes.

3. Talk with a partner about any fears or anxieties you have about speaking English. Are you afraid to make a mistake? Are you embarrassed about your English? How can you improve your confidence? Give each other ideas about how to lower your anxiety.

CHECKPOINT

How much have you learned in this unit? Review the goals for each lesson. What skills can you confidently use now? What skills do you need to practice? List these below.

Skills I've Learned Well

_____

_____

_____

_____

Skills I Need to Practice

_____

_____

_____

_____

Learning Preferences

In this unit, which type of activity did you like the best and the least? Write the number in the box: 1 = best; 2 = next best; 3 = next; 4 = least.

- ☐ Working by myself
- ☐ Working with a partner
- ☐ Working with a group
- ☐ Working as a whole class

In this unit, which exercises helped you to learn to:

listen more effectively?	Exercise _____	read more easily?	Exercise _____
speak more fluently?	Exercise _____	write more clearly?	Exercise _____

Which exercise did you like the most? _____ Why? _____

Which exercise did you like the least? _____ Why? _____

VOCABULARY

Nouns
Cold War
future
Middle East
relationship
souvenir
wedding

Past Time Expressions
last year/week/ month
years ago
yesterday

Verbs
be born
discover
explore
get engaged/ married
graduate
invent
marry
miss
pass (a course)
receive
remind
reunite
smile
stay
worry

Adjectives
adventurous
beautiful
enlarged
exciting
important
lonely
similar
sure
wonderful

Expressions
at the same time
change someone's mind
fall in love with someone
have a baby
work things out

► GRAMMAR SUMMARY

Yes/No Question and Short Responses
Did you **play** outdoors a lot?
   Yes, I did. *or* **No, I didn't.**

Information Questions and Responses
Where **did** you **go** on vacation?
   We **went** to Mexico.
When did you **leave**?
   We **left** two weeks ago.

Past Tag Questions and Short Responses
She wasn't born here, **was she**?
   Yes, she **was.** *or* **No,** she **wasn't.**
You graduated last year, **didn't you?**
   Yes, I did. *or* **No, I didn't.**

Present	Past
am, is, are	was, were
become	became
come	came
do	did
eat	ate
fall in love	fell in love
feel	felt
find	found
forget	forgot
get married	got married
go	went
has, have	had
hurry	hurried
like	liked
study	studied
tell	worried
worry	told

► COMMUNICATION SUMMARY

Sequencing events in chronological order
Poor Yon Mi! She can't decide what to do.
First, she and Han wanted to get married.
Then he changed his mind. Finally, she
decided to go to the United States to study.

Talking about the past
Yon Mi **received** a letter from her boyfriend.
Who **received** a letter from her parents?
   Yon Mi **did.**
What **did** you **do when you were a child?**
   I **played** outdoors a lot. I **went** to school.

Comparing the past with the present
Many years ago, there **were** farms here.
Today, there **are** factories.

Asking for confirmation about past events
John was born in 1973, **wasn't he?**
   Yes, he **was.** *or* **No,** he **wasn't.**
They didn't get divorced, **did they?**
   Yes, they **did.** *or* **No,** they **didn't.**

Describing historical events
Columbus arrived in America in 1492.
He started on his journey in Spain.

Talking about historical achievements
Who invented the telephone?
   Alexander Graham Bell.
When did Ts'ai Lun invent paper?
   In 105.

UNIT 3

Lesson 1

In this lesson, you will
- talk about possibility.
- invite someone by phone.
- accept and decline an invitation orally.
- leave and take a telephone message.
- write down a telephone message from an answering machine.

We could have an international fall festival!

Lynn, Nelson, and Pablo are worried about Yon Mi. They decide to have an international fall festival to cheer her up. Listen to the conversation.

Lynn: Is Yon Mi OK? I called her a few minutes ago, and she didn't want to talk.

Nelson: I don't know. She didn't come to lunch, did she? She might be homesick.

Pablo: I can understand that. I feel kind of homesick, and my family is only four hours away.

Lynn: It could be the time of year. I feel a little homesick, too.

Nelson: I miss the festival at Grandmother's in Nigeria at this time. It's a big party with dancing and singing.

Pablo: Wow, what's it called?

Nelson: The New Yam Festival.

Lynn: We also have a festival in China at this time of year. It's called the Moon Festival.

Pablo: Back home at this time of year, we celebrate "The Day of the Dead."

Lynn: The dead? It's like Halloween in the United States, isn't it?

Pablo: Yes and no. But here you are afraid of "ghosts." In Mexico, we honor our dead ancestors on this day.

Lynn: How interesting! You should give a presentation to the class about that.

Pablo: I have a better idea. Yon Mi might like it, too. We could have an international fall festival!

Pair Have you ever felt homesick? When do you usually feel homesick?

1 He might be a professor.

Look at the picture on page 25. Make guesses about the people in the coffee shop. Use *might* to express possibility.

Examples:

He might be a professor.

They might be musicians.

1. _____

2. _____

3. _____

4. _____

5. _____

Pair   Share your list with a partner. Are your guesses similar or different?

2 What might happen?

Pair   Look at the pictures. What might happen? Use *might, may, could, might not,* or *may not.*

Examples:

The man **might not** catch her.
She **could** fall.

Share your ideas with the class.

What might or could happen at the International Fall Festival? Write your predictions in your notebook. Use *might, may, could, may not,* and *might not.*

3 Can you come to the Fall Festival on Saturday?

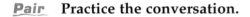 **Pablo is calling a friend. Listen to the conversation.**

Alicia: Hello?

Pablo: Hi, Alicia. This is Pablo Bonilla.

Alicia: Oh, hi, Pablo! How are you?

Pablo: Good. Hey, can we have dinner together tonight?

Alicia: Oh, sorry, I can't. I'm having dinner with my family.

Pablo: Well, can you come to the Fall Festival on Saturday?

Alicia: Sure I can. I'd love to. What time?

Pablo: I'll pick you up at 7:00.

Alicia: OK. See you then. Good-bye.

Pablo: Bye.

Pair **Practice the conversation.**

4 Can you . . . ?

Pair **Look at the cue cards and follow the instructions.**

Conversation I Student A	Conversation I Student B
1. **You are making a phone call. Start by saying "ring, ring."** 2. **Invite your friend Pam to the movies.**	1. **You are Pam. Answer the phone.** 2. **Accept Student A's invitation to the movies.**
Conversation II Student B	**Conversation II Student A**
1. **You are making a phone call. Start by saying "ring, ring."** 2. **Invite your friend Tony to your house for dinner.**	1. **You are Tony. Answer the phone.** 2. **Decline Student B's invitation to dinner. Say you are sorry and tell why you can't go.**

Present your conversations to the class. Then invent your own telephone conversations.

5 May I speak to Yon Mi, please?

🎧 **Lynn calls Yon Mi to tell her about the festival. Yon Mi isn't home, and Sook answers. Listen to the conversation.**

Sook: Hello?

Lynn: Hello. This is Lynn Wang. May I speak to Yon Mi, please?

Sook: I'm sorry. She's not here right now.

Lynn: Oh, can I leave a message?

Sook: Sure. What's the message?

Lynn: We're having a fall festival at school next Saturday. Please ask her to call me after 6 P.M.

Sook: Does she have your telephone number?

Lynn: I think so, but in case she doesn't, it's 555-0984.

Sook: OK. I'll give her the message.

Lynn: Thanks very much.

Sook: No problem.

🎧 **Now listen to Sook give Yon Mi the message. Then fill in the blanks with the missing information.**

Yon Mi: Hi, Sook. Did anyone call me?

Sook: Yes. Someone named _____.

Yon Mi: What did she want?

Sook: She wants to invite you to a _____.

Yon Mi: Did she leave a _____?

Sook: Yes, it's _____.

6 Please write down the messages from the answering machine.

🎧 **Listen to the messages on Mr. Brennan's answering machine. Mrs. Brennan has written down the first one. Complete the other messages.**

To: *Jim*	To: _____	To: *Jim*
Date: *Monday* Time: *7:00 P.M.*	Date: _____ Time: _____	Date: *Monday* Time: *7:00 A.M.*
While you were out	While you were out	While you were out
Message: *Karl called. He said he would meet you in front of the Fine Arts Museum at 8:00 A.M. tomorrow.*	Message: _____ *called.* *She said she wants you to take her to the* _____ *at* _____ *on* _____.	Message: _____ *called.* *He said you need to sign the papers for the sale of the house on* _____ *at* _____. *He'll wait for you in the* _____ *of the Transco*

Lesson 2

In this lesson, you will
- write an invitation.
- accept or decline an invitation in writing.
- talk about ongoing past activities.

You are cordially invited.

Read the invitation and replies.

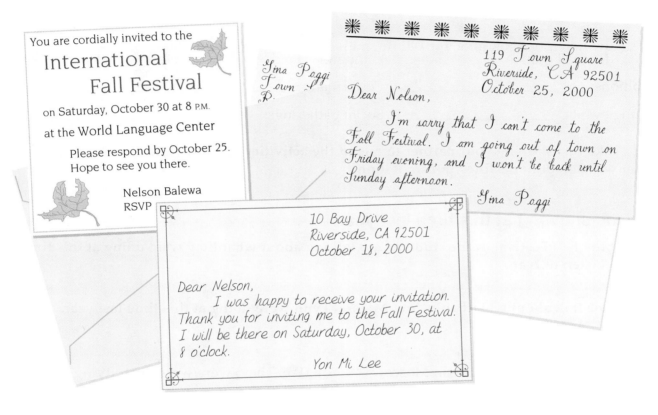

You are cordially invited to the
International
Fall Festival

on Saturday, October 30 at 8 P.M.

at the World Language Center

Please respond by October 25.
Hope to see you there.

Nelson Balewa
RSVP

Gina Poggi
Town ...
D.

119 Town Square
Riverside, CA 92501
October 25, 2000

Dear Nelson,

I'm sorry that I can't come to the Fall Festival. I am going out of town on Friday evening, and I won't be back until Sunday afternoon.

Gina Poggi

10 Bay Drive
Riverside, CA 92501
October 18, 2000

Dear Nelson,
   I was happy to receive your invitation. Thank you for inviting me to the Fall Festival. I will be there on Saturday, October 30, at 8 o'clock.

Yon Mi Lee

Pair   **Discuss the answers to these questions.**

1. Who sent the invitation?

2. What is the invitation for?

3. When and where will the event take place?

4. Who accepted the invitation?

5. Who declined the invitation? Why?

6. Why do Nelson's classmates know that an answer is expected?

Class   **Write an invitation to a school function. Give it to a classmate. In writing, accept or decline an invitation a classmate gives you.**

1 Word Bag: Leisure Activities

Pair Put each activity into one of the categories below. Add two more activities to each list.

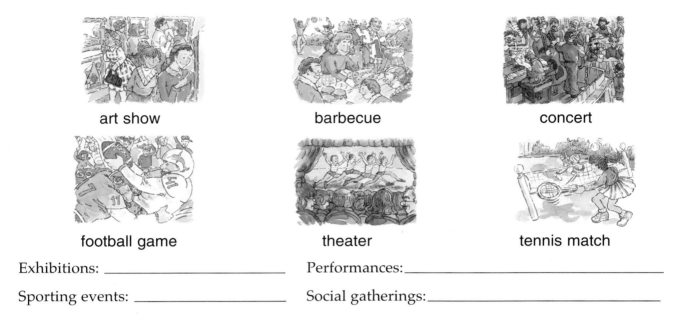

art show

barbecue

concert

football game

theater

tennis match

Exhibitions: _____   Performances: _____

Sporting events: _____   Social gatherings: _____

Pair Take turns. Invite your partner to one of the activities. Describe the activity. Your partner will accept or decline your invitation.

2 It was snowing at this time last year.

🔲 At the Fall Festival, some students are talking about what they were doing at this time last year. Listen to Ivan.

Pair Now talk about what Pablo, Yon Mi, and Lynn were doing at this time last year.

Examples:

I (He, She) **was/wasn't studying** in Moscow at this time last year.

You (We, They) **were/weren't studying** in Moscow at this time last year.

Ivan: look out / snow / wear

Pablo: have a barbecue / cook / play soccer

Lynn: attend a rock concert / sing / dance

Yon Mi and Han: go out with Han / study

3 What were you doing at this time last year?

Pair Interview your partner.

1. What were you doing at this time last year?

2. Where were you?

3. What was the weather like?

4. What were your plans for the following year?
   What did you want to do?

5. How did your plans work out?

Tell the class what your partner was doing at this time last year. In your notebook, write about what you were doing at this time last year. Use the questions above to guide you.

4 Information Gap Activity, pages 125 and 126.

Pair Turn to pages 125 and 126 and follow your teacher's instructions.

5 No, I wasn't. I was studying English.

Pair Ask your partner about what was happening three years ago.

A: **Were** you **working** three years ago?
B: Yes, I **was**. I **was working** in Tokyo.   _or_   B: No, I **wasn't working**. I **was studying** English.

1. work
2. go to school
3. live with your parents

3. study English
4. live in this city / town
5. plan to move to another city

6 Hear it. Say it.

Listen to the following words, then repeat.

Reduced Syllables

1. memory
2. mineral
3. ceremony

4. vegetables
5. separate
6. average

7. conference
8. interesting
9. favorite

Pair With a partner, practice the words in sentences of your own.

Lesson 3

In this lesson, you will
- read for general information.
- read for specific information.
- talk about the right thing to do in social situations.

Fall foods

A local chef visited the International Fall Festival. Then he wrote an article about fall foods around the world. Read the article.

>>>>>>>>>>>>>>>>>>>>>>>>>>>>>>>>

Fall Festival Foods

>>>>>>>>>>>>>>>>>>>>>>>>>>>>>>>>

When the days get shorter and the nights grow cooler, people everywhere start looking forward to the hearty foods of fall. Cooks start preparing the thick soups and special pastries that will appear at festivals.

In the United States, the season begins with Halloween. Children dress up as ghosts and scary creatures and go trick-or-treating at their neighbors' houses for candy and treats.

The Day of the Dead is a Mexican holiday celebrated the day after Halloween. People stay up all night making tamales. A tamale is a mixture of chopped meat and spices rolled in cornmeal dough, then wrapped in a corn husk and steamed. It is hard work, and the tamales must be finished before sunrise. The tamales are then placed on a special altar that honors the spirits of the dead.

In Nigeria, people celebrate the New Yam Festival with the national dish called *foofoo*. There is a special ceremony celebrating the first *foofoo* made with the new yams, and it is celebrated by lots of singing, dancing, and eating.

Many Asian countries celebrate the Moon Festival at harvest time. In Korea, for example, a special cake is made with chrysanthemum flowers. The Chinese eat moon cakes made with bean paste. The pastries are often served with warm honey water, and are a pleasant finish to a brisk walk in fall weather.

Wherever you are in the world, if it's fall, then it's probably a good time to eat and gather with friends and family.

<u>**Pair**</u>   Discuss these questions: *What kind of food do you like to eat in the fall or at harvest time? How do you make this food?*

1 The Day of the Dead is a Mexican holiday.

Pair Fill in the chart below with information from the article.

Country				Your country:	Your partner's country:
Festival					
Festival food					

2 Should we offer to pay?

🔊 **Listen to the conversation. Mr. and Mrs. Brennan, who are having coffee with some students, have left the table for a few minutes. The students don't know who should pay.**

Statement	Meaning
What should we do?	What is the right thing to do?
We should . . .	It is the right thing to do.
We shouldn't . . .	It is not the right thing to do.

Yon Mi: Mr. Brennan may expect us to pay this bill. What do you think? Should we pay the bill now?

Nelson: No, we're his guests. He might be upset if we pay it. Maybe we should wait until he comes back and then offer to pay.

Gina: He invited us. That means he should pay. We shouldn't offer.

Oscar: Well, we shouldn't offer to pay for the food because it was an invitation, but maybe we should leave a tip for the waiter.

Group Talk in groups of three or four. Who do you agree with? What would you do? Has anything like this ever happened to you? Discuss with the class.

Did you know that . . . ?
In the United States, unless someone has specifically invited you as a guest, at business-related meals, everyone pays for their own meal.

3 Online

Log onto **http://www.prenhall.com/brown_activities**
The Web: Festival fun
Grammar: What's your grammar IQ?
E-mail: Let's celebrate!

4 Wrap Up

Every culture is different. Test your knowledge of your culture and of U.S. culture. Check (✓) the boxes where the custom is practiced. Put an ✗ where the custom isn't practiced.

I am from:	In My Country	In The United States
Take your shoes off before entering the house	✓	
Bring food to a party		
Eat with your hands		
Eat with chopsticks		
Eat with a fork and knife		
Talk at the dinner table		
Sit on the floor		

Group Discuss each of the items in the chart using *should* or *shouldn't*. Start your sentences with "In my country, . . ." *or* "In the United States, . . ."

In your notebook, write a list of suggestions you might make to visitors to your country. Tell them what they should and shouldn't do in social situations. Start with the situations in the chart and add more of your own. Present your list of suggestions to the class. Compare what people should and shouldn't do in different cultures.

Strategies for Success

➤ Negotiating plans
➤ Using the telephone
➤ Reading and retelling a news story from the newspaper

1. In a group of 3–6 people, plan (a) a potluck party or (b) a trip to a local place of interest (an amusement park, a beach, a sporting event). Decide who will be responsible for what. Write an invitation. Make telephone calls to invite other guests.

2. Find a recent English language newspaper. Pick an interesting news story. Read the article, take notes on it, and prepare to tell the story to the rest of the class.

3. Tell your news story to the class.

CHECKPOINT

How much have you learned in this unit? Review the goals for each lesson. What skills can you confidently use now? What skills do you need to practice? List these below.

Skills I've Learned Well

_____

_____

_____

_____

Skills I Need to Practice

_____

_____

_____

_____

Learning Preferences

In this unit, which type of activity did you like the best and the least? Write the number in the box: 1 = best; 2 = next best; 3 = next; 4 = least.

❑ Working by myself   ❑ Working with a group

❑ Working with a partner   ❑ Working as a whole class

In this unit, which exercises helped you to learn to:

listen more effectively?   Exercise _____   read more easily?   Exercise _____

speak more fluently?   Exercise _____   write more clearly?   Exercise _____

Which exercise did you like the most? _____   Why? _____

Which exercise did you like the least? _____   Why? _____

VOCABULARY

Verbs	**Nouns**	**Adjectives**	**Expressions**
accept	altar	dead	back home
celebrate	ancestor	delicious	be afraid of
decline	barbecue	homesick	cheer someone up
invite	bill	interesting	give a presentation
offer	chef	potluck	leave a message
pay	decoration		no problem
prepare	festival	**Fall Festivals**	take off your shoes
scare	ghost	Day of the Dead	the right thing to do
turn on	guest	Moon Festival	turn on the heat (the lights)
	message	Halloween	What's wrong?
	opera	New Yam Festival	
	tip		

► GRAMMAR SUMMARY

Modals: *May, might, could, can, should*

Affirmative Statements
Tony and Nelson **may/might/could/can go** to San Francisco together.
We **should leave** a tip for the waiter.

Negative Statements
Gina **may not/might not** be here for Christmas.

People **shouldn't eat** with their hands in my country.

Yes/No **Questions**
Can you **come** to the Fall Festival?
Should we **pay** the bill?

Short Responses
Yes, I **can**. *or* **No**, I **can't**.
Yes, we **should**. *or* **No**, we **shouldn't**.

The Past Continuous Tense

Affirmative Statements
I (He, She) **was studying** English.
It **was snowing** at this time yesterday.
We (You, They) **were playing** tennis.

Yes/No **Questions and Short Responses**
Was she **watching** TV?
   Yes, she **was**. *or* **No**, she **wasn't**.

Were they **living** in the city?
   Yes, they **were**. *or* **No**, they **weren't**.

► COMMUNICATION SUMMARY

Talking about possibility
He might/may not catch her.
She could fall.

Inviting someone by phone
Can we have dinner together?

Accepting and declining invitations orally
Sure, I'd love to. What time?
Sorry, I can't. I'm having dinner with my family.

Leaving and taking a telephone message
Please ask her to call me at home after 6 P.M.
Pablo wants you to call him at 6 P.M.

Writing down a message
Karl called. He said he would meet you in front of the museum at 8 A.M. tomorrow.

Writing an invitation
You are cordially invited to a party on Saturday, October 30, at 8 P.M. at the World Language Center. Please respond by October 25.

Accepting or declining in writing
I was happy to receive the invitation. I will be there on Saturday, October 30, at 8 o'clock.

I'm sorry that I can't accept your invitation. I am going out of town.

Talking about past activities
At this time last year, I was in Moscow.

Talking about the right thing to do in social situations
Should we pay the bill now?
Maybe we should leave a tip for the waiter.

UNIT 4

Lesson 1

In this lesson, you will
- make excuses.
- discuss school policies.
- compare classroom behaviors in different cultures.

Excuses, excuses!

🔊 **Mrs. Brennan has problems with her class today. Listen to the conversation.**

Mrs. Brennan: Today we're going to talk about what we did last weekend.

Yumiko: May I join you, Mrs. Brennan?

Mrs. Brennan: Yes, you may, Yumiko. I'm glad you made it.

Yumiko: I'm sorry, Mrs. Brennan. I overslept.

Mrs. Brennan: You have to get an alarm clock, Yumiko. Let's get started. Last weekend, I was working in the yard, and I got thirsty.

Ivan: Hello, everybody! I'm sorry I'm late, Mrs. Brennan. I ran out of gas. I was driving, and my car stopped.

Mrs. Brennan: Ivan, you mustn't interrupt the class like this. Sit down, please.

Ivan: There isn't any room. I'll just sit over here.

Mrs. Brennan: No, we can make room. Tony, can you move to the left?

Tony: I can't, Mrs. Brennan. I have to sit in a warm place because I have a cold.

Mrs. Brennan: Yumiko, please trade places with Tony. Back to my story. I got a big glass of iced tea . . .

Oscar: Good morning, sorry I'm late.

Mrs. Brennan: Yes, Oscar. Please sit down. As I was saying, I was admiring the flowers, and I didn't notice a bee on my glass. I took a big drink, and . . .

Ivan: What are we doing today?

Mrs. Brennan: We're going to talk about the things you must and mustn't do in class!

Pair Are you ever late for class or appointments? If so, what do you say? What do you do? Do you know someone who is always late? How does it make you feel?

1 Word Bag: Making Excuses

People make excuses when they come to an appointment late or when they have to leave early. When would you use each of the following excuses? Complete each excuse with *I'm sorry I'm late* or *Sorry, I have to leave.*

1. _____.
I have a date.

2. _____.
I have a doctor's appointment.

3. _____.
I have to pick up my kids.

4. _____.
I have to study for an exam.

5. _____.
I had to take my son to school.

6. _____.
I missed the bus.

Did you know that . . . ?
In the United States, punctuality is highly valued. Call if you're going to be late.

2 I'm sorry. I missed the train.

Listen to the conversations.

A: You're late. I've been waiting for an hour.
B: I'm sorry. I missed the train.

A: Lunch was great. Do you want more coffee?
B: Sorry, I can't. I have to get back to work.

Pair **Role play these situations.**

1. Student A and Student B are meeting for dinner, but Student B is two hours late. Student A complains, and Student B makes an excuse.

2. Student A and Student B are having a business meeting. Student B wants to continue, but Student A has to leave and makes an excuse.

3 Information Gap Activity, pages 125 and 126.

Pair **Turn to pages 125 and 126 and follow your teacher's instructions.**

4 Students must not eat in class.

Every culture has appropriate and inappropriate classroom behaviors. Read the chart below.

> Students **have to**/**must** stand up when the teacher arrives. (It is necessary.)
>
> Students **don't have to** raise their hands before asking questions. (It is not necessary.)
>
> Students **must not**/**mustn't** eat in class. (It is against the rules.)

Group In a group of four, discuss these classroom behaviors in your countries and in the United States. Write *true* if the statement is true, *false* if it is false.

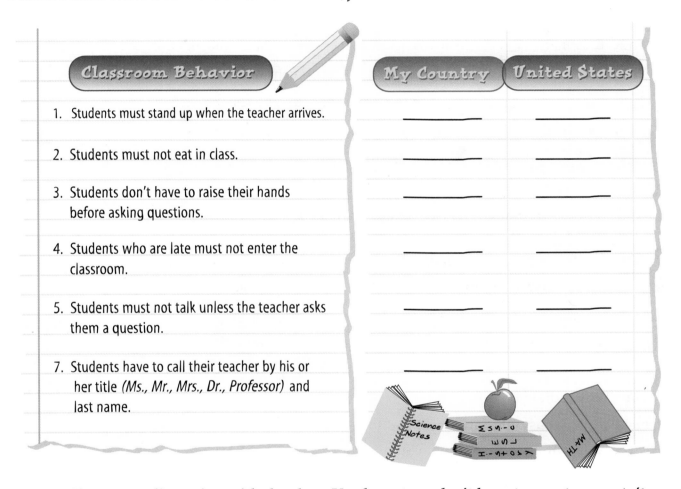

Classroom Behavior | **My Country** | **United States**

1. Students must stand up when the teacher arrives.

2. Students must not eat in class.

3. Students don't have to raise their hands before asking questions.

4. Students who are late must not enter the classroom.

5. Students must not talk unless the teacher asks them a question.

7. Students have to call their teacher by his or her title *(Ms., Mr., Mrs., Dr., Professor)* and last name.

Class Share your discussion with the class. Use *have to* or *don't have to, must* or *mustn't,* and *may* where appropriate.

Example:

In my country, students **must** stand when they speak in class, but in the United States students **don't have to**.

5 What's the school policy?

Pair   Read the school policies below. Fill in the blanks with *may* or *mustn't*.

A student **may** discuss homework with another student. (It is not against the rules.)

A student **must not** discuss homework with another student. (It is against the rules.)

Policies on Student Academic Honesty

1. A student _____ ask another what the homework assignment is.

2. A student _____ lend his homework to another student to copy.

3. A student _____ do his or her homework in class while the teacher is teaching.

4. A student _____ ask another student for help with test instructions.

5. A student _____ ask an instructor for help with test instructions.

6. A student _____ look at other students' papers during a test.

Class   Discuss your answers. On the board, make a list of your school's policies.

6 Can I copy your homework?

Listen and read. Complete the sentences with the correct object pronouns.

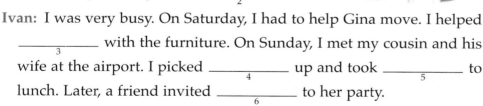

Ivan: Did you do your homework?

Nelson: Yes, I did. How about you?

Ivan: I didn't have time to do _____.
      1

Nelson: Why didn't you do _____?
      2

Ivan: I was very busy. On Saturday, I had to help Gina move. I helped _____ with the furniture. On Sunday, I met my cousin and his
      3
wife at the airport. I picked _____ up and took _____ to
      4   5
lunch. Later, a friend invited _____ to her party.
      6

Nelson: What are you going to do about your homework now?

Ivan: Can I look at yours and copy _____?
      7

Nelson: It's not a good idea, Ivan. Mrs. Brennan told _____ not to do that.
      8

Ivan: But she doesn't have to know if you don't tell _____.
      9

Nelson: I think you should explain it to _____. She'll understand why you didn't do your
      10
homework.

PRONOUNS	
Subject	**Object**
I	me
you	you
he	him
she	her
it	it
we	us
they	them

In this lesson, you will
- identify personality types.
- identify abilities and talents.
- discuss personal and academic goals.
- make predictions about the future.

You value creativity.

Yon Mi is giving a presentation on personality types to the class. Look at the picture.

You might be all of these types. But usually one type is strongest.

The Innovator: You value creativity and challenge. When you work in a group, you love to solve problems, but sometimes you like to work independently. You sometimes take great risks.

The Socializer: You value your relationships with others. When you work in a group, you listen well and encourage others. People want to work with you.

The Thinker: You value learning. When you work in a group, you ask a lot of questions, and you want to know the reason for everything. People come to you for information.

The Organizer: You value order. When you work in a group, you always follow directions and pay attention to details. You are often the most stable person in a group.

Class **Do you think knowing your personality type can help you at school or at work? How?**

1 If you value relationships . . .

Pair Read the descriptions and identify the personality type. Write *Socializer*, *Organizer*, *Thinker*, or *Innovator* after each description.

Yumiko: I love to draw and take pictures. Sometimes, I take my camera and walk around the city. Then, I mix the pictures with my drawings. I enjoy figuring out new ways to make pictures. _____

Nelson: I collect maps. As a result, I know a lot about geography. The more I learn about the world, the more I want to know. When I work in a group, my classmates ask me questions because I know a lot. _____

Tony: I like to study languages because I like to figure out the rules. I do all my homework, and I'm prepared for tests. I like to know that I am writing or speaking correctly. _____

Lynn: I enjoy spending time with my family. My older brothers and sisters are married now, and I call them all the time. At family parties, I don't mind cooking and cleaning up. I like to take care of people. _____

2 What's your personality type?

Write the personality type that is most like you and the one that is the least like you.

Most like: _____   Least like: _____

Pair Now find a partner who has the same "most like" personality type as you have. Ask your partner these questions.

1. Why are you a/an _____? Can you give an example?

2. What do you usually enjoy doing when you work in a group?

3. What do you like other people to take care of when you work with them?

4. Do you think it's better to work with someone who is similar or different? Why?

In your notebook, write a paragraph describing your personality.

3 I'm going to exercise more.

Before each new year, people think about their goals for the following year. These goals are called resolutions. Here are some resolutions. Put a check (✓) before any goals that will help you become a better person and student. Then write two more goals in each column.

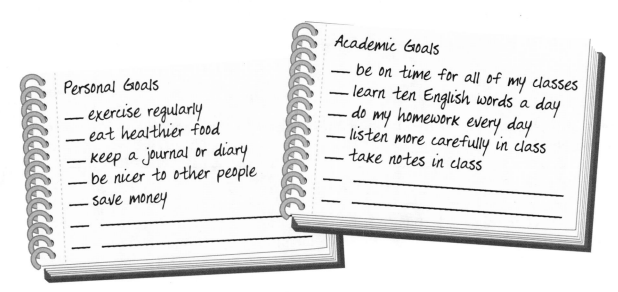

Personal Goals
— exercise regularly
— eat healthier food
— keep a journal or diary
— be nicer to other people
— save money
— _____
— _____

Academic Goals
— be on time for all of my classes
— learn ten English words a day
— do my homework every day
— listen more carefully in class
— take notes in class
— _____
— _____

Pair   Now compare your goals with a partner's. Report your partner's goals to the class. Write your personal goals in paragraph form in your notebook.

Examples:

  I'm going to exercise more.   He's/She's going to study more.

4 Where are you going to live?

Pair   Ask your partner these and other questions. Write down his or her answers. Then write what kind of job you think he or she might have in the future.

1. Where are you going to live?

2. What are you going to do in your free time?

3. Are you going to work for a company, or have your own business?

Report your prediction to the class. Give reasons for your prediction.

5 Hear it. Say it.

Listen to the words. Check (✓) the word you hear.

Minimal Pairs [b] [p]

1. [ ] bad   [ ] pad   4. [ ] bees   [ ] peas   7. [ ] ban   [ ] pan

2. [ ] lab   [ ] lap   5. [ ] cab   [ ] cap   8. [ ] lib   [ ] lip

3. [ ] rib   [ ] rip   6. [ ] cub   [ ] cup

Pair   With a partner, practice pronouncing the pairs of words.

Lesson 3

In this lesson, you will
- complete a learning style questionnaire.
- discuss learning styles.
- write about future goals.

What is your learning style?

What type of learner are you? Complete the questionnaire to find out. For each statement, circle a number.

3 = a lot like you	2 = a little like you	1 = not at all like you
I learn better when the teacher writes on the board. 3 2 1	I learn better when the teacher gives a lecture. 3 2 1	I learn better when I do things in class. 3 2 1
I write things down so I can remember them. 3 2 1	I say things out loud so I can remember them. 3 2 1	I role-play things so I can remember them. 3 2 1
Before I read, I look at the pictures. 3 2 1	I like to read aloud. 3 2 1	I like to act out what I am reading. 3 2 1
I like to study in a quiet place. 3 2 1	I like to study with music. 3 2 1	I like to move around when I study. 3 2 1
I like to learn from diagrams and charts. 3 2 1	I like to learn from cassettes and CDs. 3 2 1	I like to learn from experiments. 3 2 1
I like to take notes when the teacher is talking. 3 2 1	I like to ask the teacher questions. 3 2 1	I like to help the teacher organize field trips. 3 2 1
Total	**Total**	**Total**
VISUAL	**AUDITORY**	**KINESTHETIC**

Now add up the numbers in each column. The column with your highest score indicates the type of learner you are.

Pair   Find a partner who is a different kind of learner. Compare your answers to the quiz.

1 I like to talk about my experiences.

Group   Are these people visual, auditory, or kinesthetic learners? Write the reasons for your choice. Discuss your ideas with a group.

1. My name is Alice Ditmore. I like computers. I learn best when I can look at charts and diagrams. I enjoy math and physics, and I like to see how things work. I'm going to be an engineer.

Reasons: _____

_____

2. My name is John Pappas. I like to move around a lot. In a classroom, I like to explore new ideas and learn about other places. I enjoy traveling. I'm going to become a pilot.

Reasons: _____

_____

3. My name is Jean Kasuga. I like to spend time with my friends, and I like to talk about my experiences. In class, I like to have group discussions. I ask many questions. I'm going to be a teacher.

Reasons: _____

_____

2 Classroom activities for your learning style

Group   Work with two or three classmates who have the same learning style as you do. Make a list of classroom activities that fit your learning style. Use the examples to get you started.

Visual	Auditory	Kinesthetic
Make a poster with drawings of new vocabulary.	Write and perform a song using new vocabulary.	Go to a cafe and practice speaking English.

Class   Present your list of activities to the class. Explain why these activities fit your learning style. Take notes on the activities of groups with different learning styles.

3 Online

Log onto **http://www.prenhall.com/brown_activities**
The Web: The perfect job
Grammar: What's your grammar IQ?
E-mail: What's your talent?

4 Wrap Up

What are you going to be doing ten years from now? Write three goals for your future. Then write what you have to do to reach each goal.

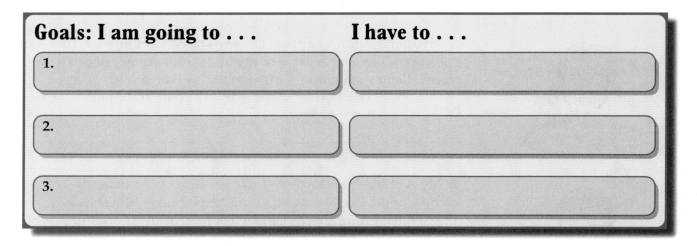

Goals: I am going to . . .	I have to . . .
1.	
2.	
3.	

Pair Talk to your partner about his/her goals. Suggest other things he/she has to do to reach each goal. Add your partner's suggestions to your chart.

Using your ideas and your partner's ideas, write a paragraph about your goals and what you have to do to reach them.

Strategies for Success

➤ **Analyzing yourself**
➤ **Discovering characteristics of successful language learners**
➤ **Describing your own personality**

1. With a different partner than the one you worked with in class, compare your results of the Learning Style Inventory in Lesson 3. Talk about your similarities and differences.

2. With that same partner, identify things you can do outside of class to help you to be stronger in the two learning styles that were **not** your highest score.

3. In your journal, describe yourself in the words used in the Learning Style Inventory. Then, answer the question "Is there anything I should change about myself in order to be a more successful learner?"

CHECKPOINT

How much have you learned in this unit? Review the goals for each lesson. What skills can you confidently use now? What skills do you need to practice? List these below.

Skills I've Learned Well

_____

_____

_____

_____

Skills I Need to Practice

_____

_____

_____

_____

Learning Preferences

In this unit, which type of activity did you like the best and the least? Write the number in the box: 1 = best; 2 = next best; 3 = next; 4 = least.

☐ Working by myself   ☐ Working with a group

☐ Working with a partner   ☐ Working as a whole class

In this unit, which exercises helped you to learn to:

listen more effectively?	Exercise _____	read more easily?	Exercise _____
speak more fluently?	Exercise _____	write more clearly?	Exercise _____

Which exercise did you like the most? _____   Why? _____

Which exercise did you like the least? _____   Why? _____

VOCABULARY

Verbs	Nouns	Adjectives	Expressions
collect	appointment	academic	I'm glad you made it!
drive	behavior	appropriate	pay attention to
encourage	cassette, CD	independent	run out of gas (time)
interrupt	challenge	necessary	take care of
oversleep	creativity	personal	take notes
pick up	diagram	stable	trade places with
role-play	experience		turn in (homework)
share	experiment	**Personality Types**	
solve	field trip	innovator	**Learner Types**
stand up	lecture	organizer	auditory
value	reason	socializer	kinesthetic
	risk	thinker	visual

► GRAMMAR SUMMARY

Modals: *Have to/Had to/Must*

Affirmative Statements
I (You, We, They) **have to/had to/must** study.

She (He) **has to/had to/must** study.

Negative Statements
I (You, We, They) **don't have to/didn't have to** study.
She (He) **doesn't have to/didn't have to** study.

Yes/No Questions
Do I (you, we, they) **have to** study for the test?
Did I (you, we, they) **have to** study for the test?

Does she (he) **have to** study for the test?
Did she (he) **have to** study for the test?

Short Responses
Yes, I (you, we, they) **do/did.**
No, I (you, we, they) **don't/didn't.**

Yes, she (he) **does/did.**
No, she (he) **doesn't/didn't.**

Modals: *Must, May*

Affirmative Statement
I **must** go to the library.
I **may** ask another student about the test.

Negative Statement
I **must not/mustn't** be late for class.

Future with *Going to*

Yes/No Questions
Am I going to study more?
Is he (she) **going to** study more?
Are we (you, they) **going to** study more?

Short Responses
Yes, you **are.** *or* **No,** you **aren't.**
Yes, he (she) is. *or* **No,** he (she) **isn't.**
Yes, we (you, they) **are.** *or* **No,** we (you, they) **aren't.**

► COMMUNICATION SUMMARY

Making an excuse
I'm sorry I'm late. I overslept.

Comparing classroom behaviors in different cultures/Reading about and discussing school policies
Students must not eat in class.
Students may discuss homework assignments.

Identifying personality types/Identifying abilities and talents
I love to solve problems, but sometimes I like to work independently. I think I'm an innovator.

Talking about personal and academic goals
I'm going to exercise more. I'm going to learn ten English words a day.

Making predictions about the future
I think you're going to be a teacher.

Discussing learning styles
I role play things so I can remember them, and I like to learn from experiments. I'm a kinesthetic learner.

Lesson 1

In this lesson, you will
- talk about places in a neighborhood.
- compare two places in a town or city.
- ask for and give directions.

Is this the way to the festival?

Look at the picture as you listen.

Lynn: What a pretty town! It's prettier than Los Angeles.

Yon Mi: Yes, and it's cleaner than L.A., too. I bet we're already close to the ocean. I can smell it. I think the festival is this way.

Oscar: No, it's on Laguna Canyon Road.

Tony: Laguna Canyon Road runs the other way.

Lynn: You're holding the map the wrong way. The festival is closer than you think.

Oscar: Hey, guys. Look at those people. They're walking *that* way. Do you think they're going to the festival?

Yon Mi: Let's ask someone. I don't want to miss anything. Excuse me sir, is this the way to the festival?

Lynn: Yon Mi, he's a mime. Mimes never talk. They communicate with gestures.

Yon Mi: I know. But look, he's pointing.

Tony: Wait a second. He's gesturing "Go down this street, pass through two lights and turn left, um, next to . . . next to . . . sick people," next to a hospital!

Yon Mi: Are you sure, Tony?

Tony: Trust me. I'm a visual learner, so I'm good with mimes.

Yon Mi: Yes, Tony, you may be better with mimes than I am, but where's the festival?

Lynn: It's OK, Yon Mi, I see a sign. The festival is straight ahead.

Pair **Did you ever have problems when you tried to find a new place? Tell your partner about what happened.**

1 Word Bag: The Neighborhood

Pair   Look at the map. Label the buildings and places.

Now listen to the conversations. Write where the activities are taking place.

1. _____the bank_____
2. _____
3. _____
4. _____
5. _____
6. _____

Did you know that . . . ?
In the United States, you can borrow current video and audiocassettes of best-selling books from town libraries. Libraries also offer a wide range of activities for children and adults.

2 In My Neighborhood

Group   Discuss the following.

1. Does your neighborhood look like the one in the map? What is similar? What is different?

2. Is there a library in your neighborhood? Do you have a library card? Do you like to study in the library? Why or why not?

3. How often do you go to the post office? What services does it provide? How long does it take to send a letter from your country to other countries?

4. What other places in your neighborhood do you go to often? Why?

In your notebook, write a paragraph about your favorite place in your neighborhood. Describe it and tell why it is your favorite.

3 Getting Around

🔊 **Student A is at the aquarium. Listen to the directions as you look at the map.**

A: Excuse me. How do I get to the bank?

B: Walk east on Park Avenue for three blocks. Turn left on Pine Street. Walk north for two blocks and turn right on Laguna Canyon Road. Walk along Laguna Canyon Road to Maple Street. The bank is on the corner of Maple Street and Laguna Canyon Road, across from the police station.

Pair **Work with a partner. Ask for and give directions:**

1. from the post office to the Seaside Hotel.
2. from the park to the Laguna Beach Festival.
3. from the museum to the movie theater
4. from the library to the park.
5. from the bank to the Laguna Grille.
6. from the baseball field to the library.

4 Turn right at Laguna Canyon Road?

🔊 **Listen to the directions and check (✓) where you are on the map.**

1. [ ] baseball field
2. [ ] library
3. [ ] bank

[ ] Laguna Grille
[ ] museum
[ ] police station

5 Life in a small town is safer than life in a big city.

Pair   Look at the picture. Use the adjectives in the box. Compare life in a small town and life in a big city.

cheap→cheaper	expensive→more/less expensive	good→better
quiet→quieter	exciting→more/less exciting	bad→worse
noisy→noisier	interesting→more/less interesting	

Example:

A: Life in a small town is safer than life in a big city.

B: Yes, but life in a big city is more exciting. Small towns are less interesting than big cities.

6 Joe's Café is better than Harry's Grille.

Group   Compare places in your city or town. First write the names of two places in the chart. Then decide which place is better and give reasons.

Example:

Joe's Café is better than Harry's Grille because it's less crowded and the food is fresher.

Place	Name #1	Name #2	Reasons
1. bank			
2. supermarket			
3. shopping mall			
4. park			
5. movie theater			
6. school			

Report your choices to the class. In your notebook, compare two more places in your city or town.

Lesson 2

In this lesson, you will
- read for specific information.
- talk about holidays.
- talk about past habits and customs.

Come to the Winter Fantasy Festival.

Read about the Winter Fantasy Festival.

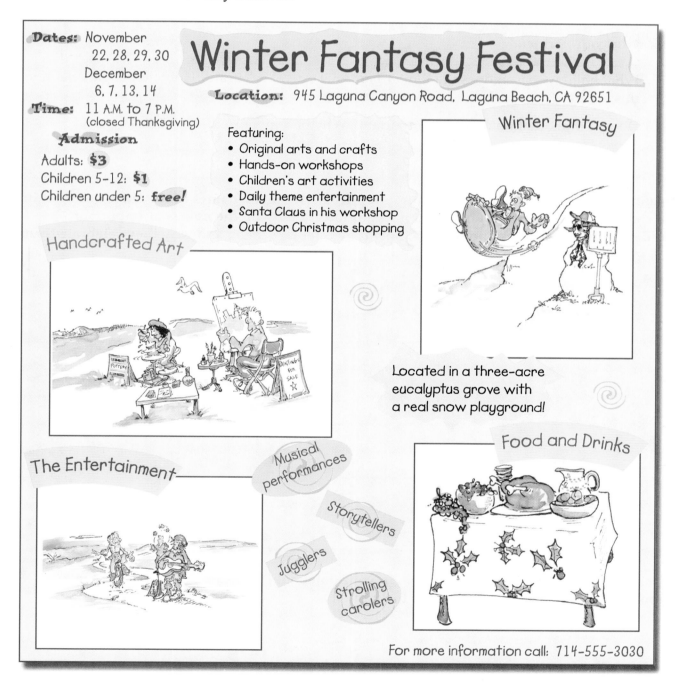

Dates: November 22, 28, 29, 30 December 6, 7, 13, 14

Time: 11 A.M. to 7 P.M. (closed Thanksgiving)

Admission
Adults: **$3**
Children 5-12: **$1**
Children under 5: **free!**

Winter Fantasy Festival

Location: 945 Laguna Canyon Road, Laguna Beach, CA 92651

Featuring:
- Original arts and crafts
- Hands-on workshops
- Children's art activities
- Daily theme entertainment
- Santa Claus in his workshop
- Outdoor Christmas shopping

Winter Fantasy

Handcrafted Art

Located in a three-acre eucalyptus grove with a real snow playground!

The Entertainment

Musical performances

Storytellers

Jugglers

Strolling carolers

Food and Drinks

For more information call: 714-555-3030

1 Winter Fantasy Festival

Pair   Check (✓) the correct answers.

1. The Winter Fantasy Festival is held in

    [ ] Laguna.   [ ] Laguna Beach.

2. People can shop for gifts at the Festival.

    [ ] true   [ ] false

3. Everyone has to pay the price of admission.

    [ ] true   [ ] false

4. The Festival is held during

    [ ] one month.   [ ] two months.

5. The Festival closes on a holiday.

    [ ] true   [ ] false

6. The festival opens at 7 A.M.

    [ ] true   [ ] false

Talk with your partner.

1. What holiday season does the Winter Fantasy Festival celebrate? How do people celebrate this holiday?

2. Do you think that holidays are important? Why or why not?

2 Holiday Survey

Group   **Where are the students in your group from? Write the names of the cities or towns in the chart. Ask students from different backgrounds to tell you the names of important holidays, when people celebrate them, how they celebrate them, and why they celebrate them.**

	City	Holiday	When?	How?	Why?
1.					
2.					
3.					
4.					

Discuss your chart with the class. Then, in your notebook, write a paragraph about an important holiday celebration in your town or city.

3 I used to trim the tree in the evening.

Look at the examples.

> I **used to** trim the tree in the evening.
>
> I **didn't use to** wrap the gifts.
>
> **Did** you **use to** wrap the gifts?
>
>   Yes, I **did**. *or*
>
>   No, I **didn't**. My mother **used to** wrap them.

Complete the conversation with the correct form of the verbs. Use *use to* and *used to* when appropriate.

A: I _____ in Grand Rapids, but now I live in Los Angeles.
    1. live

B: Where in Grand Rapids _____?
    2. you/live

A: My parents _____ the old Mill Town farm. But I really _____ it there.
    3. rent   4. like/not

B: Why not?

A: Well, we didn't have any neighbors or relatives nearby, so we _____ the
    5. spend
    holidays alone. I _____ the Christmas tree, but there was nobody to see it.
    6. trim
    And we didn't have electricity, so the tree _____ any lights.
    7. have/not

B: _____ make Christmas dinner?
    8. you/help

A: Yes, I _____ the turkey, and my sister _____ the pies.
    9. stuff   10. bake

Pair   How did you use to spend Christmas or another holiday when you were a child? Talk
with your partner about all the things you used to do. Then write a paragraph about how you
used to celebrate the holiday.

4 Hear it. Say it.

🔊   **Listen to the words. Check (✓) the word you hear.**

Minimal Pairs [b] [v]

1. [ ] ban   [ ] van   5. [ ] habit   [ ] have it
2. [ ] best   [ ] vest   6. [ ] bow   [ ] vow
3. [ ] boat   [ ] vote   7. [ ] robe   [ ] rove
4. [ ] berry   [ ] very   8. [ ] curb   [ ] curve

Pair   **With a partner, practice pronouncing the pairs of words.**

Lesson 3

In this lesson, you will
- write a journal entry.
- describe differences between two cities.

Yon Mi's Journal

Read Yon Mi's journal entry.

November 25

We're back in Riverside. I was more homesick yesterday than today. Yesterday I felt so sad I wanted to jump on the next flight to Pusan. But today, I think that my decision to come to the U.S. was a good one. I'm having experiences that I'll remember for the rest of my life.

We went through Los Angeles on our way back to Riverside. L. A. is bigger and shinier than my little town, but it also seems lonelier. People don't know each other, and they seem to be always in a hurry. We went to Hollywood and drove by the houses of some movie stars in Beverly Hills. We didn't get out of the car. There wasn't anyone walking on the street. The houses were big and beautiful, but the neighborhood was empty.

It made me appreciate Pusan more. Back home when I used to walk or ride my bike, I always used to see familiar faces on the streets. I used to stop and talk to people almost every time I went out. Everyone used to know everybody else. We used to know where everyone lived and the history of everyone's families.

I don't know if people in big cities like Los Angeles have the same feeling of home that we do. I think big city people move a lot, and they often live next to strangers. I used to think that living in Hollywood would be very exciting and glamorous. But there's one thing in small towns that big cities like Los Angeles or Hollywood will never have—a sense of community.

In your journal, write about your feelings and experiences. Start by writing about the city or town where you are living now and comparing it with a city or town where you used to live.

1 My city is bigger than your city!

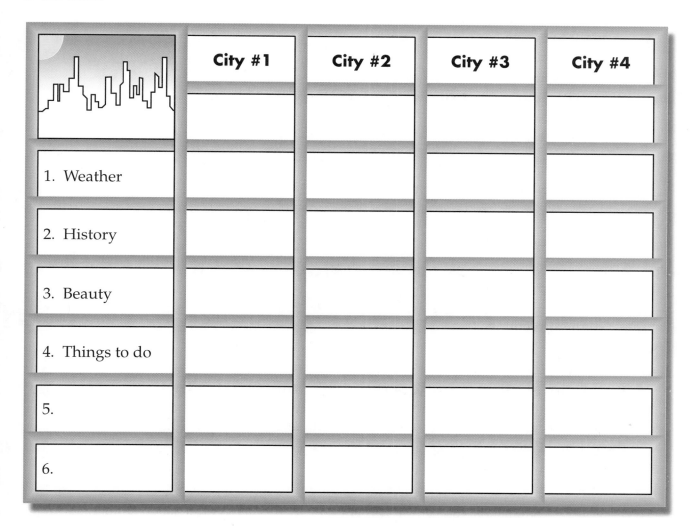

Listen to the cassette. Then read the sentences and write T (true) or F (false).

1. __T__   The weather in Los Angeles is better than the weather in Mexico City.
2. _____   Mexico City is less polluted than Los Angeles.
3. _____   Mexico City is older than Los Angeles.
4. _____   The history of Los Angeles is more interesting than the history of Mexico City.
5. _____   Barcelona is smaller than Los Angeles and Mexico City.
6. _____   Lynn thinks Hong Kong is both old and new.

Group   In a group of three or four, compare your home cities or towns. Compare the things listed below and add others that are interesting to you. Present the results of your discussion to the class.

	City #1	City #2	City #3	City #4
1. Weather				
2. History				
3. Beauty				
4. Things to do				
5.				
6.				

2 Information Gap Activity, pages 127 and 128.

Pair   Turn to pages 127 and 128 and follow your teacher's instructions.

3 My Town

<u>Pair</u>   **Ask your partner these questions, and add questions of your own.**

1.   Do you prefer a big city with busy street life or a small, quiet town near nature?

2.   Do you want to be in a place near the water? an ocean or a river?

3.   Do you like an older city with lots of history and interesting architecture or a modern city with newer buildings and lots of growth?

In your notebook, write a paragraph suggesting a city or town where your partner would enjoy living. Explain why you suggest it.

4 Online

Log onto **http://www.prenhall.com/brown_activities**
The Web: Comparing information about cities
Grammar: What's your grammar IQ?
E-mail: My town

5 Wrap Up

<u>Group</u>   **Work with your group to design the perfect city. First, discuss these questions.**

1.   What is the climate like? Is it hilly? near water? near mountains?

2.   What is the population? What do most of the people do? What are the main jobs?

3.   What is the city famous for? What do tourists like to visit?

Give your city a name. Next, draw a picture of your city on a piece of paper. Then write a description of the city. Describe your city to the class.

Strategies for Success

➤ **Giving directions**
➤ **Writing to use comparatives**
➤ **Reviewing your goals**

1. With a partner, find a map of your city or town. Choose a place on the map. Take turns giving each other directions to a "secret" place you choose, such as a restaurant several miles away. Without pointing, tell your partner how to get there. Can he or she find it?

2. Write about a festival or holiday in your country. Use comparatives to describe the festival. For example, "The dancing is more fun than the singing."

3. Look back at the goals you set for yourself in Unit 1. Have you reached some of them? Should you change some of them? Should you try harder? Write your thoughts in your journal.

CHECKPOINT

How much have you learned in this unit? Review the goals for each lesson. What skills can you confidently use now? What skills do you need to practice? List these below.

Skills I've Learned Well

_____

_____

_____

_____

Skills I Need to Practice

_____

_____

_____

_____

Learning Preferences

In this unit, which type of activity did you like the best and the least? Write the number in the box: 1 = best; 2 = next best; 3 = next; 4 = least.

- ☐ Working by myself
- ☐ Working with a partner
- ☐ Working with a group
- ☐ Working as a whole class

In this unit, which exercises helped you to learn to:

listen more effectively?   Exercise _____   read more easily?   Exercise _____

speak more fluently?   Exercise _____   write more clearly?   Exercise _____

Which exercise did you like the most? _____   Why? _____

Which exercise did you like the least? _____   Why? _____

VOCABULARY

Verbs	Nouns	Adjectives	Expressions for Directions
appreciate	admission	available	around the corner
celebrate	decision	empty	block
communicate	eucalyptus	familiar	cross
hold	festival	far	close to
point	gift	glamorous	east, north, south, west
prefer	mime	modern	How can I get to . . . ?
seem	mountain	polluted	on the left (right)
smell	nature	safe	opposite
stop	pollution	straight	straight ahead
walk	stranger	unique	this/that way
wrap	tourist		

► GRAMMAR SUMMARY

Forming the Comparative of Adjectives

Regular Adjectives

One-syllable Adjectives	Comparative Form (Adjective + -er)
hard	harder
sad	sadder

Two-syllable Adjectives Ending in -y	Comparative Form (Adjective + -er)
easy	easier
busy	busier

Multi-syllable Adjectives	Comparative Form (more/less + adjective)
beautiful	more/less beautiful
difficult	more/less difficult

Irregular Adjectives

Adjectives	Comparative Form
good	better
bad	worse
far	farther/further
much/many	more
little/few	less

Used to

Affirmative Statement
I (you, she, he, we, they) **used to** walk in the park.

Negative Statement
I (You, He, She, We, They) **didn't use to** walk in the park.

Yes/No Question and Short Responses
Did I (you, she, he, we, they) **use to** walk in the park?
   Yes, I (you, she, he, we, they) **did.** *or*
   No, I (you, she, he, we, they) **didn't.**

► COMMUNICATION SUMMARY

Talking about places in a neighborhood
My favorite place is the library. It is quiet there, and I love to read.

Asking for and giving directions
How can I get to Arlington Street from here?
   Go down the street and turn left.

Comparing two places in a town or city
Joe's Café is better than Harry's Grille because it's less crowded and the food is fresher.

Talking about holidays
We celebrate our new year on March 21.

Talking about past habits and customs
We used to trim the Christmas tree in the evening. My sister used to bake pies, and I used to stuff the turkey.

Writing a journal entry
I was more homesick yesterday than today. Yesterday I felt so sad that I wanted to go home.

Describing differences between two cities
Los Angeles is more polluted than Riverside. My hometown is smaller than Houston.

UNIT 6

Lesson 1

In this lesson, you will

- talk about health problems and remedies.
- make suggestions.
- make a doctor's appointment.
- give advice.

Don't try to talk with that sore throat.

Lynn, Tony, Oscar, and Yon Mi are at the local clinic. They all returned sick from the festival. Look at the picture. Then listen as you read the conversation.

Lynn: I hope we don't have to wait too long. I really feel sick. Tony, don't scratch!

Tony: I can't help it. My leg itches.

Oscar: You have poison oak. Put butter on it.

Lynn: It's probably only ant bites. Rub a raw potato on your skin.

Tony: Yon Mi, don't try to talk with that sore throat. Write it down here.

Yon Mi: (writing) *I think you have ant bites. Mix baking soda and water and put it on your skin.*

Tony: What's this? Do you want to cook me or cure me?

Nurse: Lynn, the doctor will see you now. The rest of you can fill these out.

Doctor: What seems to be the matter?

Lynn: I have chills and a headache.

Doctor: Are you nauseated?

Lynn: Yes, very. And I'm thirsty, too.

Doctor: Uh-oh. . . Did you eat a hamburger at the Festival?

Lynn: How did you know?

Doctor: Because I've already seen half-a-dozen patients with the same symptoms. You have food poisoning, and I know what probably caused it.

Lynn: The hamburger?

Doctor: Right. Drink a lot of water and get some rest. Call me tomorrow.

Pair   Have you ever tried a home remedy to cure a simple ailment? What did you use? Did it work? Tell your partner about this home remedy.

1 What do you do to stay healthy?

Pair Discuss the following questions.

1. Have you ever had any of the illnesses mentioned in the conversation? Which one(s)?

2. When was the last time you were sick? What did you or your family do?

3. What do you do to stay healthy?

4. What do you do when you get sick?

Report your partner's answers to the class.

2 Word Bag: Ailments and Treatments

Group Decide which treatments or remedies are good for each of these ailments or injuries.

Example:

You **should** cover a cut with a Band-Aid.

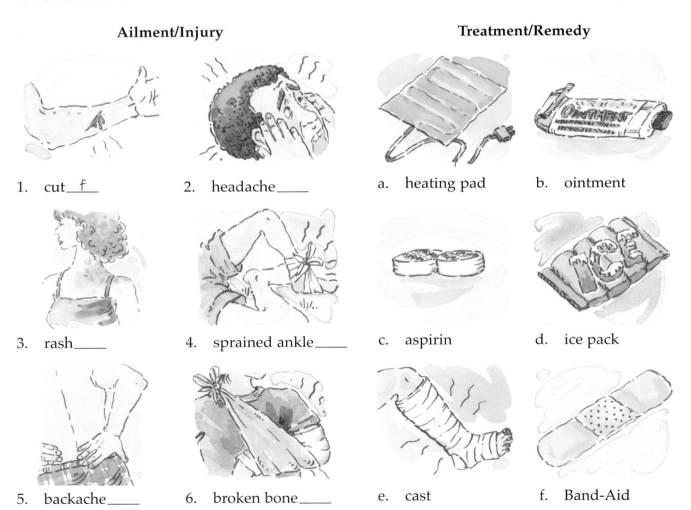

Ailment/Injury

Treatment/Remedy

1. cut _f_

2. headache____

3. rash____

4. sprained ankle____

5. backache____

6. broken bone____

a. heating pad

b. ointment

c. aspirin

d. ice pack

e. cast

f. Band-Aid

Report your decisions to the class.

3 I need to see a doctor.

Below is the list of specialists and their available days and times at a local clinic.

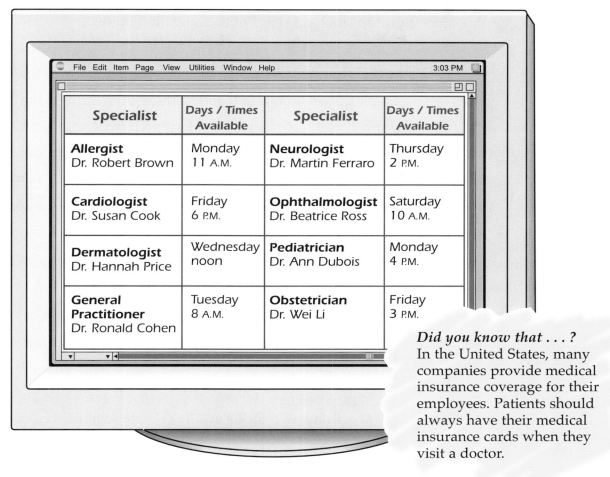

Specialist	Days / Times Available	Specialist	Days / Times Available
Allergist Dr. Robert Brown	Monday 11 A.M.	**Neurologist** Dr. Martin Ferraro	Thursday 2 P.M.
Cardiologist Dr. Susan Cook	Friday 6 P.M.	**Ophthalmologist** Dr. Beatrice Ross	Saturday 10 A.M.
Dermatologist Dr. Hannah Price	Wednesday noon	**Pediatrician** Dr. Ann Dubois	Monday 4 P.M.
General Practitioner Dr. Ronald Cohen	Tuesday 8 A.M.	**Obstetrician** Dr. Wei Li	Friday 3 P.M.

Did you know that . . . ?
In the United States, many companies provide medical insurance coverage for their employees. Patients should always have their medical insurance cards when they visit a doctor.

Pair Choose from the list of problems below.

1. Your baby has a fever and isn't eating.
2. You get headaches when you watch TV.
3. You get out of breath when you walk up a flight of stairs.
4. You need a medical check-up to renew your insurance.
5. You have a rash, and your skin is itchy.
6. Your hands get numb when you work at the computer.
7. You sneeze a lot around cats.
8. Your sister is pregnant.

Your partner is a receptionist at a doctor's clinic. Call the clinic to make an appointment, and tell your partner what your problem is. He or she will tell you which doctor you need to see. Switch roles.

A: Community Clinic. Can I help you?
B: Yes. I **need to see** a doctor.
A: What's the matter?
B: Well, I sneeze a lot and my eyes water.

A: Oh, then you **want to see** an allergist. Dr. Brown can see you on Monday at 11:00 A.M. **Would** you **like to make** an appointment?
B: Yes, please.

4 He agreed to go to the doctor.

Complete the paragraph with infinitives from the list.

> He agreed **to stop** smoking.   I offered **to help** him.

to follow   to give   to go   to help   to see   to smoke   to stop   to work

My friend Mark agreed _____ smoking. He hated _____ it up, but I
offered _____ him. I recommended a specialist, but Mark preferred _____
his general practitioner. The doctor told Mark to eat candy every time he wanted _____.
Mark decided _____ the doctor's advice. It seemed _____, but it caused
another problem. Now Mark needs _____ to the dentist!

**Has a doctor ever given you advice? What was the advice? Did you follow it? If so, what did
you do? If not, what did you decide to do instead? Write a paragraph in your notebook.**

5 Dear Doctor . . .

<u>Group</u>   **Read the letters below. Decide together what advice you can give each writer. Write
two pieces of advice below each letter.**

Dear Doctor,
    I am always tired. I usually get eight hours of sleep
each night, but it doesn't help. What should I do?
                                        Pooped Out

Dear Pooped Out,
1. _____

    _____

2. _____

    _____

Dear Doctor,
    My problem is this: I can't sleep
at night. I go to bed at 10 P.M., but
I never fall asleep before 3 A.M. I
get up for work at 6 A.M., and I
need more sleep. What can I do?
                        Sleepless

Dear Sleepless,
1. _____

    _____

    _____

2. _____

    _____

    _____

Dear Doctor,
    I want to lose 20 pounds. I've tried many diets, but I
just can't loose weight. I need some advice—fast!
                                        Too Chubby

Dear Too Chubby,
1. _____

    _____

2. _____

    _____

Read your advice to the class.

Lesson 2

In this lesson, you will

- discuss a healthy diet.
- talk about preferences, likes, and dislikes in food.
- plan a balanced meal.
- listen to advice and take notes about a healthy diet.

A Healthy Diet

How much do you know about a healthy diet? Take the quiz. Start with box 1.

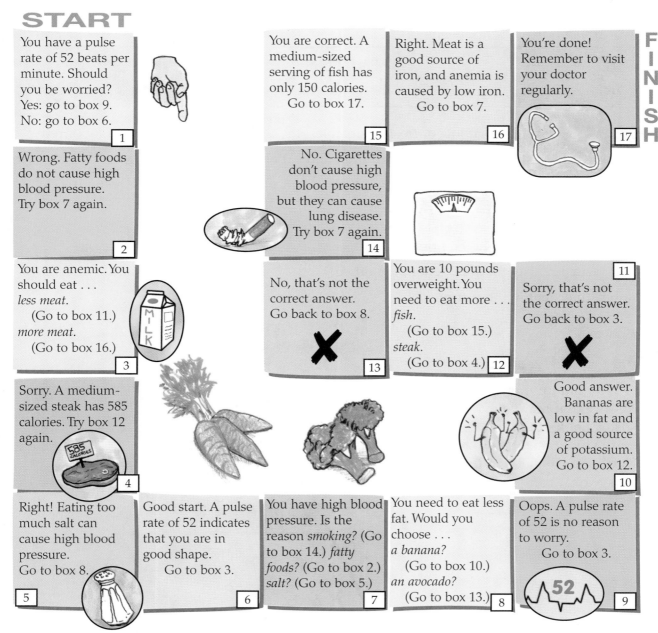

START

1 You have a pulse rate of 52 beats per minute. Should you be worried? Yes: go to box 9. No: go to box 6.

15 You are correct. A medium-sized serving of fish has only 150 calories. Go to box 17.

16 Right. Meat is a good source of iron, and anemia is caused by low iron. Go to box 7.

17 You're done! Remember to visit your doctor regularly.

FINISH

2 Wrong. Fatty foods do not cause high blood pressure. Try box 7 again.

14 No. Cigarettes don't cause high blood pressure, but they can cause lung disease. Try box 7 again.

3 You are anemic. You should eat . . . *less meat.* (Go to box 11.) *more meat.* (Go to box 16.)

13 No, that's not the correct answer. Go back to box 8.

12 You are 10 pounds overweight. You need to eat more . . . *fish.* (Go to box 15.) *steak.* (Go to box 4.)

11 Sorry, that's not the correct answer. Go back to box 3.

4 Sorry. A medium-sized steak has 585 calories. Try box 12 again.

10 Good answer. Bananas are low in fat and a good source of potassium. Go to box 12.

5 Right! Eating too much salt can cause high blood pressure. Go to box 8.

6 Good start. A pulse rate of 52 indicates that you are in good shape. Go to box 3.

7 You have high blood pressure. Is the reason *smoking?* (Go to box 14.) *fatty foods?* (Go to box 2.) *salt?* (Go to box 5.)

8 You need to eat less fat. Would you choose . . . *a banana?* (Go to box 10.) *an avocado?* (Go to box 13.)

9 Oops. A pulse rate of 52 is no reason to worry. Go to box 3.

<u>Pair</u>   **Discuss:** *What is a healthy diet? What kinds of foods do healthy people eat?*

1 I try to eat lots of fresh vegetables.

boil   fry   steam   bake   broil

Complete the paragraph with words from the box or the labels under the pictures. Try to use as many of the words as possible.

like/love/hate	try/try not	forget/remember
prefer/don't like	plan/would like	healthy/not so healthy

I _____ to eat lots of fresh vegetables. I _____ to eat a lot of red
_____1_____   _____2_____

meat. I _____ to drink enough milk and eat enough cheese. I _____ to
        _____3_____   _____4_____

eat a great deal of junk food such as ice cream, cake, and potato chips. Most of the time, I

_____ to eat fruit for snacks.
_____5_____

In terms of cooking methods, I prefer to _____, _____, or
                                          _____6_____   _____7_____

_____ my food. In general, my diet is _____ . I _____ to
_____8_____   _____9_____   _____10_____

have a healthier diet in the future.

2 The Food Pyramid

Pair   The food pyramid shows the
type of diet that many doctors think
is healthy. Look at the food pyramid.
Compare your answers in Exercise 1.
Which of you has the healthier diet?
Discuss.

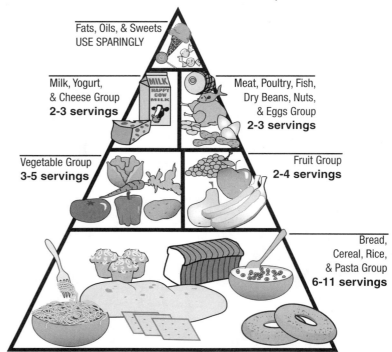

Fats, Oils, & Sweets
USE SPARINGLY

Milk, Yogurt,
& Cheese Group
2-3 servings

Meat, Poultry, Fish,
Dry Beans, Nuts,
& Eggs Group
2-3 servings

Vegetable Group
3-5 servings

Fruit Group
2-4 servings

Bread,
Cereal, Rice,
& Pasta Group
6-11 servings

3 Do you eat to live or live to eat?

Mixer   First, answer these questions. Use the same questions to find three or four classmates who have the same eating habits you do.

1. Do you like to eat food that tastes good or food that is good for you? Is food important to you?

2. Do you like to read recipes and articles about food and cooking, or do you prefer to experiment?

3. Do you take time to plan your meals, or do you prefer to eat whatever is in the refrigerator?

Group   Work with your group to plan a meal. Think about what you want to eat, how to cook it, and what you need to buy. Describe your meal to the class.

4 At the Health Food Store

Ivan and Nelson have decided to get in shape. They visit a health food store and ask the clerk about a healthy diet. Listen to the conversation and complete Nelson's notes. Write *Don't* in front of things they should not do. Check (✓) the things they should do.

```
1.  Don't  eat a lot of red meat.    6. _____ use a lot of butter.
2. _____ eat a lot of vegetables.  7. _____ eat white bread and rice.
3. _____ boil vegetables.          8. _____ eat whole grains.
4. _____ steam vegetables.         9. _____ eat a lot of dairy products.
5. _____ use olive oil.           10. _____ eat fruit.
```

5 Hear it. Say it.

Listen to the sentences. Circle (S) for statement or (Q) for question.

Statement or Question?

1. They wanted to eat healthy food S Q	4. They shouldn't eat much butter S Q
2. They went to a health food store S Q	5. They should steam the vegetables S Q
3. They didn't know where to begin S Q	6. They need to eat fruit every day S Q

Practice with a partner. Read each sentence above, first as a statement, then as a question. Use only intonation to show the difference.

6 Information Gap Activity, pages 129 and 130.

Pair   Turn to pages 129 and 130 and follow your teacher's instructions.

Lesson 3

In this lesson, you will

- read an article about alternative medicine.
- discuss health problems and remedies.
- write a short report.

Alternative Medicine

When you are sick, do you go to a doctor? Read the article to find out what people worldwide do when they are sick.

Alternative Medicine

Do you massage the back of your head to cure a headache? Do you put an ice pack on a sprained ankle? Do you listen to the radio to keep calm during a traffic jam? If your answer to any of these questions is "yes," then you are practicing alternative medicine.

Before modern medicine, people used plants and home remedies to cure ailments. In general, alternative medicine is based on six main points:

1. People have a natural ability to heal. The body's healing power is more important than technique and technology.

2. The patient is more important than the doctor. The doctor works with the patient's feelings, beliefs, and opinions when deciding on a treatment.

3. Aggressive therapies may harm the patient. Alternative medicine uses techniques and therapies with few or no side effects.

4. Healing takes time. The body's natural healing response, unaided by medicine, takes longer, but there is less chance for the symptoms to return.

5. Natural and whole ingredients work. Many alternative treatments use herbs, plants, nutritional supplements, and whole foods. Drugs may be quicker and more effective, but they often come with unpleasant side effects.

6. The whole person must be treated. Doctors look at the whole person, not just the part that is sick. Doctors include the body and the mind in deciding on a cure.

Pair   Discuss with your partner.

1. What are the main differences between alternative and modern medicine?

2. Which of the six points above do you agree with? Which don't you agree with? Why?

3. Do you think alternative medicine is helpful? Why or why not?

1 Plants as Preventive Medicine

Many plants have good effects on our health. Read these descriptions of six plants. Learn how they can prevent some common and serious illnesses.

Garlic is used as an ingredient in food all over the world. It may lower blood pressure and cholesterol and thin the blood. Some research shows that garlic may help to treat stomach ulcers.

Ginger is another food commonly used in cooking. Ginger is one of the best remedies for a cold. Some people also use this plant to relieve motion sickness and dizziness.

Bananas are grown in hot climates. Some people eat bananas to fight colds. People also eat bananas for indigestion and heartburn.

Tea is one of the most popular drinks around the world. Some people drink it for indigestion. In Japan, green tea is used to prevent tooth decay. In many Asian countries, people believe that oolong tea can reduce cholesterol level and lower blood pressure.

People all around the world eat oranges, a source of vitamin C. Our skin and other tissues need vitamin C to stay healthy. Vitamin C-rich foods protect us from cold germs.

Chili peppers are very popular in many countries, such as Mexico, Colombia, India, and Thailand, where chilies make a variety of foods spicy. Chilies are used as remedies for flu and headaches. They may also slow the development of some types of cancer.

Eating Healthy   78

Pair   Discuss with your partner the plants you could use for the following ailments: colds, high cholesterol, indigestion, high blood pressure, flu, headache, stomach ulcers, cancer.

2 Online

Log onto **http://www.prenhall.com/brown_activities**
The Web: Staying healthy
Grammar: What's your grammar IQ?
E-mail: Get well soon!

3 Wrap Up

Group Each health problem in the chart has a suggested remedy. In a group of three, discuss the problem and the suggested remedy. Suggest two more remedies for each. Then add two more health problems and two remedies for each one.

Health Problem	Suggested Remedy	Your Remedies
a cold	Drink a lot of tea and juices.	_____
a headache	Rub some chili peppers on your forehead.	_____
a toothache	Put clove oil on your teeth.	_____
puffy eyes	Put wet tea bags on your eyes.	_____
a burn	Put aloe vera on the burn.	_____
a sprain	Put ice on the sprain.	_____
insomnia (trouble sleeping)	Drink warm milk before going to bed.	_____
	_____	_____
	_____	_____

Write a short report based on your discussion.

Strategies for Success

➤ Recycling vocabulary and phrases about health
➤ Creating opportunities to practice English
➤ Writing about an illness or accident

1. With a partner, talk about healthy lifestyles: what you both think you should do to be healthy people, such as getting plenty of sleep, eating a balanced diet, and exercising regularly. Make a list of "ten commandments" for a healthy lifestyle. Put your list on a wall or bulletin board.

2. With some classmates, go to a restaurant that serves "health food." Order items that you think are especially healthy: low-fat, whole-grain, low-sugar, etc. Talk about your orders with each other in English.

3. In your journal, describe a time when you were sick or had a bad accident. Share your story with a partner and/or the rest of the class.

CHECKPOINT

How much have you learned in this unit? Review the goals for each lesson. What skills can you confidently use now? What skills do you need to practice? List these below.

Skills I've Learned Well

_____

_____

_____

_____

Skills I Need to Practice

_____

_____

_____

_____

Learning Preferences

In this unit, which type of activity did you like the best and the least? Write the number in the box: 1 = best; 2 = next best; 3 = next; 4 = least.

☐ Working by myself   ☐ Working with a group

☐ Working with a partner   ☐ Working as a whole class

In this unit, which exercises helped you to learn to:

listen more effectively?   Exercise _____   read more easily?   Exercise _____

speak more fluently?   Exercise _____   write more clearly?   Exercise _____

Which exercise did you like the most? _____   Why? _____

Which exercise did you like the least? _____   Why? _____

VOCABULARY

Verbs	Nouns	Medical Specialists	Ailments & Remedies	
advise	advice	allergist	alternative	high blood
cure	ailment	cardiologist	medicine	pressure
experiment	cure	dermatologist	anemia/ anemic	injury
fry	health food	general	ant bites	nauseated
get in shape	illness	practitioner	bandage	ointment
itch	junk food	neurologist	cast	poison oak
prescribe	pulse	obstetrician	checkup	pregnant
renew	remedy	ophthalmologist	dizzy	sprained ankle
rub	symptom	pediatrician	food poisoning	
scratch	treatment		heart disease	
sneeze	weight		herbs	
steam	whole food			
weigh				

▶ GRAMMAR SUMMARY

Verbs Followed by Infinitives			Examples
agree	love	remember	I **need to see** a doctor.
forget	need	try	They **like to steam** fresh vegetables.
hate	plan	want	She **plans to eat** healthier food in the future.
like	prefer	would like	

Modal: *Should* (Review)

Affirmative Statement
You **should go** to the doctor.

Negative Statement
You **shouldn't eat** junk food.

Affirmative and Negative Imperatives (Review)

Affirmative Imperatives	Negative Imperatives
Eat healthy food.	**Don't eat** a lot of junk food.
Drink a lot of juice when you have a cold.	**Don't forget** to take your pills.
Get a lot of rest and drink a lot of water.	**Don't try** to talk with a sore throat.

▶ COMMUNICATION SUMMARY

Talking about health problems and remedies
I think I'm catching a cold. I have a sore throat and a headache.
In my country, people put butter on poison oak.
You should use a Band-Aid on that cut.

Making a doctor's appointment
I need to see a doctor.
I'd like to make an appointment with Dr. Sanders, please.
Dr. Brown can see you on Monday at 11:00.
Would you like to make an appointment?
   Yes, please.

Making suggestions/giving advice
You should exercise more.
Don't eat before sleeping.

Discussing a healthy diet
People should try to eat 3 to 5 servings of vegetables a day.

Talking about preferences, likes, and dislikes in food
I prefer to eat some kind of meat for dinner.
I don't like fish very much.
Yoshi likes to have yogurt and fruit for breakfast, but I prefer milk and cereal.

Planning a balanced meal
I'd like to broil some fish.
We need to add some vegetables.
We shouldn't use a lot of butter.

Writing a report on health problems and remedies
Doctors often suggest that you drink a lot of tea and juices when you have a cold. Ana also likes to get a lot of rest, and Ali says that you should eat a lot of chili peppers.

Lesson 1

In this lesson, you will
- talk about purchases.
- write a letter of complaint.
- exchange a purchase.
- compare features of stores.

I planned to buy the smallest TV in the store.

Ivan bought a TV set. Listen and read about the problem he had with the TV.

Nelson: Ivan, why did you buy this big TV?

Ivan: Well, I planned to buy the smallest TV in the store . . .

Nelson: This is the smallest TV?

Ivan: I asked for the smallest one, but the salesman said a big TV is the best choice.

Oscar: This is the biggest TV I've ever seen!

Ivan: Do you think I made a mistake? It was on sale.

Oscar: Well, a small TV is cheaper than this big TV, and a small TV is easier to move!

Tony: There are lots of persuasive salespeople, so you have to be careful when you go shopping.

Ivan: I guess he got a nice commission.

Tony: Yep, he's probably laughing all the way to the bank.

Pair Discuss the conversation with your partner. Do you think it is dangerous to deal with an aggressive salesperson? How can shoppers protect themselves?

1 I would like to return an item.

Ivan is returning the TV set. Listen to the conversation.

Ivan: Hello. May I speak to the manager?

Manager: This is the manager. How may I help you?

Ivan: I would like to return a TV set I bought this morning.

Manager: May I know why you want to return the TV?

Ivan: It's too big for my apartment.

Manager: Here's what you should do. Write a letter to the Customer Service Department, and attach the receipt.

Ivan: Yes, I'll do that. Thank you.

Pair Discuss: Is Ivan's reason for returning the TV set valid? Explain.

2 To Whom It May Concern

Ivan wrote a letter of complaint to the store where he bought his TV. Complete the sentences with *and*, *but*, *or*, or *so*.

Examples:

It was a good price, **and** it was on sale.

The TV was nice, **but** it was too big.

You can pay cash, **or** you can charge it.

It was inexpensive, **so** I bought it.

December 15, 2000

A.J. Gerlain's Department Store
Customer Service Department
565 First Avenue East
Riverside, California 98002

To whom it may concern,

I would like to return the TV set that I bought from your store. I wanted to get a smaller TV for my apartment, _____ a salesman at your store sold me a much larger one.
₁
He was very convincing, _____ I bought the biggest set that he showed me. The TV
₂
wouldn't fit in my car, _____ I had to rent a bigger one. It is now in my apartment,
₃
_____ I can't find a place to put it.
₄

Could you give me a refund, _____ could I choose a smaller replacement? Enclosed
₅
is a copy of the receipt. Could your delivery truck pick up the TV? Thank you for your prompt attention.

Sincerely,

Ivan Gorki

Pair You ordered shoes from a catalog but would like to return them. On a piece of paper, write a letter to the Customer Service Department explaining why you're returning them.

3 I bought this yesterday, and I'd like to exchange it.

Listen to three customers complain about things they bought at Gerlain's Department Store. Write what they want to exchange, why they want to exchange it, and how the problem is resolved.

Customer	What?	Why?	How?
1.			
2.			
3.			

Group In a group of three, make a list of reasons people return purchases. Share your list with the class.

4 Our toys are the cheapest.

Pair Complete the ad with the superlative form of the adjectives.

cheap ➤ cheaper ➤ the cheapest	expensive ➤ more expensive ➤ the most expensive
big ⟶ bigger ⟶ the biggest	bad ⟶ worse ⟶ the worst
busy ➤ busier ⟶ the busiest	good ⟶ better ⟶ the best

TOY TOWN—*The Biggest Toy Store in Texas*

Come to **TOY TOWN** and see (1)_____ and
(new)

(2)_____ toys in town! Our dolls are
(exciting)

(3)_____! Our bicycles are (4)_____!
(pretty)   (cheap)

Our video games are (5)_____! Our selection is
(good)

(6)_____, and our prices are (7)_____!
(wide)   (low)

5 Computer World is the best.

Mr. Brennan is writing a story about computer stores for a local magazine. Look at his notes and then answer the questions.

	Salespeople	Selection	Prices
Computer World Open daily except Sundays 10 A.M. to 9 P.M.	Friendly, mostly college students.	Large: all brands of laptop and desktop computers, printers, modems, and CD-ROMs.	Very expensive. Finance rate: 15%
The Input Open Monday to Friday 8:30 A.M. to 6 P.M.	Very friendly, with degrees in computer science.	Small: only some brands of desktop computers and printers. No laptops, modems, or CD-ROMs.	Expensive. Finance rate: ~ 5%
Computer Central Open daily 9 A.M. to 11 P.M.	Unfriendly, but with at least 5 years computer sales experience.	Large selection of some brands of laptop and desktop computers, printers, modems, and CD-ROMs.	Cheap. Finance rate: 15%

1. Which computer store has the most convenient hours? _____

2. Which one has the friendliest salespeople? _____
   Which has the most experienced salespeople? _____

3. Which one has the largest selection? _____

4. Which one has the best prices? _____
   Which has the lowest finance rate? _____

Pair Discuss which computer store is the best for you. Write a paragraph comparing the three stores. Use the questions above to guide you.

_____

_____

_____

_____

_____

_____

_____

Lesson 2

In this lesson, you will
- compare features of items.
- make a catalog purchase.
- give reasons for returning a purchase.

I don't have enough cash.

Did Gina get a good deal? Listen to and read the following conversation.

Lynn: I like those wool sweaters.

Gina: Yes, and they're a good deal! I also love the red dress.

Clerk: Your total is $114.79.

Lynn: Doesn't she get a discount? That sign on the wall says 25 percent off all purchases over a hundred dollars.

Clerk: Yes, but the discount doesn't apply to sale items. Your non-sale purchases alone total $74.86.

Gina: So if I buy something else, can I get the discount?

Clerk: Yes, we have some lovely silk skirts. They go with the sweaters you just bought.

Gina: Oh, these aren't as expensive as the wool skirts, are they?

Clerk: No, they aren't. With the skirt and the discount, the total would be about $116.

Gina: That's a great deal. Uh-oh . . .

Lynn: What?

Gina: I don't have enough cash. I have to use my mom's credit card. Oh well, she won't mind when I tell her how much money I saved on today's sale.

Lynn: Hmm . . . I wonder if you saved as much money as Ivan did yesterday.

Gina: OK, OK, I didn't exactly save money, but it was still a good deal!

Pair Was it a good idea for Gina to use her mother's credit card? What do you think Gina's mother will say? Have you ever made a bad shopping decision? Tell your partner what happened.

1 Word Bag: Stores

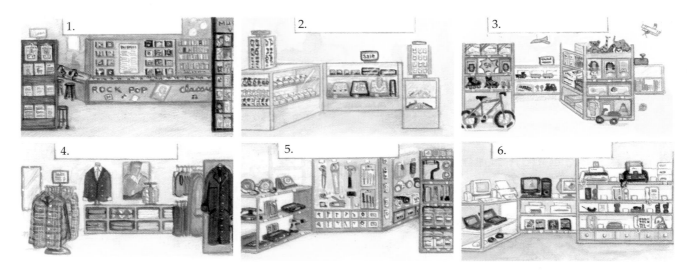

Pair Write the name of each store in the box above each picture: Clothing, Toys, Electronics, Hardware, Jewelry, Music. Write the number of the store that sells each of the items below. Add two more items, then write the number of the store that sells them.

[5] nails   [ ] doll   [ ] fax machine   [ ] necklace

[ ] computer [ ] videocassette   [ ] wristwatch   [ ] shirt

[ ] bicycle   [ ] sheet music   [ ] screwdriver   [ ] hammer

[ ] CDs   [ ] cell phone   [ ] _____   [ ] _____

2 Is the black dress as elegant as the blue dress?

Pair Compare each pair of items below, using the adjectives under each picture.

The black dress is **more elegant** than the blue dress.

The black dress is **as elegant** as the blue dress.

The blue dress is **not as elegant** as the black dress.

elegant

fast

fashionable

convenient

Group Compare and discuss your answers with your group and report back to class. With your group, choose two things: two cars, two schools, two places. On a piece of paper, write a paragraph comparing the two things you chose.

3 The Style Quiz

Pair Ask your partner the questions and circle his or her answers.

1. At a party, you see a person wearing the same clothes as you. What do you do?
   (a) Leave the party.
   (b) Compliment the person.
   (c) Pay no attention because you're having so much fun.

2. When you buy shoes and clothes, what influences your decision?
   (a) Current fashion.
   (b) Fit and price.
   (c) Need.

3. When you are invited to a formal wedding, what do you wear?
   (a) A formal outfit bought especially for the occasion.
   (b) Formal clothes that you have worn before.
   (c) Whatever you find hanging in your closet.

4. Are you going to buy a new jacket?
   (a) Yes, yours is out of style.
   (b) No, yours is still in good condition.
   (c) Yes, your old one is worn out.

5. You're at a nice restaurant waiting for your sister. She arrives wearing shorts and a wrinkled shirt. How do you feel?
   (a) Embarrassed.
   (b) Disappointed.
   (c) It doesn't bother you.

Score your partner's answers:
   (a) Fashion is important to you. You work hard to look good.
   (b) You are practical. You try to look good, but you don't spend a lot of time and money on shopping and clothes.
   (c) Fashion does not matter to you. You have other interests that take your time and energy.

Group In a group of four, compare and discuss the results of the quiz. How important is fashion to you? to your partner? in your culture? Why?

In your notebook, write a paragraph about fashion and how important it is in your country.

4 Information Gap Activity, pages 131 and 132.

Pair Turn to pages 131 and 132 and follow your teacher's instructions.

5 Hear It. Say it.

Listen to the words. Check (✓) the word you hear.

Minimal Pairs [b] [d]

1. [ ] bad   [ ] dad
2. [ ] bed   [ ] dead
3. [ ] big   [ ] dig
4. [ ] pebble   [ ] pedal

5. [ ] robes   [ ] roads
6. [ ] web   [ ] wed
7. [ ] herb   [ ] heard
8. [ ] tribe   [ ] tried

Pair With a partner, practice pronouncing each pair of words.

In this lesson, you will
- analyze information in an advertisement.
- write an advertisement.

Can you save money when you spend money?

🔊 **Read and listen to the advertisement. Would you enroll in the *Everyday Rewards* program?**

The UNICA Card®

If you're not enrolled in the *Everyday Rewards* program,

call 1-800-REWARDS

and start earning points immediately.

Five everyday ways to faster rewards.

You make purchases almost every day–you buy groceries, fill up the car, mail packages, or buy stamps. Now you can turn all the purchases you make into rewarding experiences. Just use a *Unica Card* instead of cash or checks.

Look at these everyday places where your purchases can add up to points and rewards:

- at the grocery store
- at the post office
- at the department store
- at entertainment and sports events

How? For every dollar you charge on your *Unica Card*, you will earn valuable points that can be credited toward gifts, travel, hotel discounts, and other rewards. So think about using the *Unica Card* this holiday season.

Group Discuss these questions.

1. What product is advertised?

2. Who are the customers for this product? Young people? Parents? Retired people? Rich people? People who need to save money?

3. What do you think of the Unica Card? Is it useful? Would you use it?

4. Should you believe advertisements? Why or why not?

1 What are they selling?

Pair What do you think each ad is selling? Discuss with your partner.

"We eat as much as we can and sell the rest."   "The best comes from a tiny mountain village."

Group In a group of four, discuss the two ads. Are the ads effective in attracting customers?

2 It could happen to you.

Group A scam is a trick to get someone's money. In groups, discuss what you could do in these situations. Make a list of suggestions for avoiding these scams.

Gold Card Scam

A woman phones to offer you a low-interest credit card. To process the card, she needs some information from you. This will be your first gold credit card, so you are excited and give her the information she asked for.

You never get the card. Later, you discover that the caller used the information to steal from your bank account and used your credit card.

The Slippery Used-Car Dealer

You want to buy a used car. The dealer shows you a car and says that it is in perfect condition. You are happy with the test drive, so you buy the car.

A week later, you notice sand in the carpet. Your mechanic tells you the car was in a flood and the metal is rusting away.

Paying for Your "Prize"

You get a sweepstakes notice in the mail. It says you have won a valuable prize. To learn how to collect, you must call a special long-distance number.

When you call, the person talks to you a long time. Finally he says that you must pay shipping charges for your "prize." You hang up—but they've already charged you for the expensive phone call.

Quick-Change Artist

You are watching a musician play the guitar on the street. A man asks you for change. He shows you a twenty-dollar bill. You give him a ten, a five, and five one-dollar bills. The man puts a dollar in the musician's hat and leaves.

You look at the money in your hand and find that you are holding a one-dollar bill.

3 Online

Log onto **http://www.prenhall.com/brown_activities**
The Web: Shopping on the Internet
Grammar: What's your grammar IQ?
E-mail: Shopping spree

Did you know that . . . ?
Shopping on the Internet is rapidly increasing. Every year more and more sales are made over the Internet.

4 Wrap Up

Group **Work in a group of four. You have a language school. Design an advertisement for your school.**

1. Circle the type of market you are targeting: (You can circle more than one.)

   K-6   **Middle School**   **High School**   **Adults**   **Seniors**

2. Check the media you will advertise in.

   _____ radio   _____ television   _____ newspapers

   _____ magazines   _____ flyers   _____ other:_____

3. Write a catchy slogan for your school:

   _____

4. Write a 30-second commercial or design a flyer for your language school.

5. Present your commercial or flyer to the class.

Strategies for Success

➤ **Role playing business transactions**
➤ **Using television for listening practice**
➤ **Writing to persuade**

1. Find a mail-order catalog written in English. Decide on ten items that you would like to order. With a partner, role play the process of ordering the items.

2. Make plans to listen to an English-speaking television program that has commercials in it. Listen very carefully for words (for example, "more," "discount," "sale"), phrases (for example, "number one," "save more money"), and superlatives ("best," "the most efficient") that try to convince you to buy a product. Write a paragraph about whether this commercial was convincing.

3. Write a description of a particular product that you would like to own, such as a special model of a car, a particular type of computer, or a stereo system. Describe why you think this product is (a) important for you to have, and (b) the best choice compared to other models. Read your description aloud to your partner.

CHECKPOINT

How much have you learned in this unit? Review the goals for each lesson. What skills can you confidently use now? What skills do you need to practice? List these below.

Skills I've Learned Well

_____

_____

_____

_____

Skills I Need to Practice

_____

_____

_____

_____

Learning Preferences

In this unit, which type of activity did you like the best and the least? Write the number in the box: 1 = best; 2 = next best; 3 = next; 4 = least.

- ☐ Working by myself
- ☐ Working with a partner
- ☐ Working with a group
- ☐ Working as a whole class

In this unit, which exercises helped you to learn to:

listen more effectively?   Exercise _____   read more easily?   Exercise _____

speak more fluently?   Exercise _____   write more clearly?   Exercise _____

Which exercise did you like the most? _____   Why? _____

Which exercise did you like the least? _____   Why? _____

VOCABULARY

Verbs
advertise
apply
bother
carry
complain
exchange
fit
influence
load
purchase
return
save

Stores
clothing
electronics
hardware
jewelry
music
toy

Nouns
cash
cell phone
comfort
commission
complaint

cotton
discount
fax machine
flyer
hammer
item
nail
necklace
product
purchase
raincoat
scam

screwdriver
selection
service
silk
sports jacket
style
wool
wristwatch

Adjectives
aggressive
anxious

attractive
convenient
dangerous
efficient
elegant
expensive
experienced
persuasive
reasonable
valid
worn out

▶ GRAMMAR SUMMARY

Compound Sentences

		Conjunction	
Additional information: *and*	It was a good price,	**and**	it was on sale.
Contradictory information: *but*	The TV was nice,	**but**	it was too big.
Alternate information: *or*	You can pay cash,	**or**	you can charge it.
Result: *so*	It was expensive,	**so**	I didn't buy it.

Forming the Superlative of Adjectives

Regular Adjectives

One-syllable Adjectives

big ⟶ the biggest
cheap ⟶ the cheapest

Two-syllable Adjectives Ending in -*y*

busy ⟶ the busiest
heavy ⟶ the heaviest

Multisyllable Adjectives

beautiful ⟶ the most beautiful
expensive ⟶ the most/least expensive

Irregular Adjectives

good ⟶ the best
bad ⟶ the worst
far ⟶ the farthest

Comparisons of equality with *as . . . as*

	Subject	Verb *Be*	*as* + adj.+ *as*	Complement
Affirmative	The black dress	is	as elegant as	the blue dress.
Negative	The wool skirts	are not	as fashionable as	the silk ones.

▶ COMMUNICATION SUMMARY

Talking about purchases
It was on sale.

Writing a letter of complaint
I wanted to buy a small TV, but the salesman sold me a large one.

Exchanging a purchase
I bought this yesterday, and I'd like to exchange it.

Comparing features of stores
Computer Central has the lowest prices.

Comparing features of items
The black dress is more elegant than the blue dress, but it is also more expensive.

Giving reasons for returning a purchase
I'd like to return this shirt because it doesn't fit. I have one just like it.

Analyzing information in an advertisement
I think this advertisement is for adults.

Writing an advertisement
It's the fastest way to learn English.

Lesson 1

In this lesson, you will
- talk about budgets.
- talk about actions that have already happened.

Have you paid the tuition bills yet?

Gina's parents are having dinner together. Read and listen to their conversation.

Mrs. Poggi: I'm so proud of the kids. Alberto is in college, and now Gina is going to start. By the way, have you paid the tuition bills yet?

Mr. Poggi: I paid the car insurance, the electric bill, and Alberto's tuition, but I haven't paid Gina's tuition yet.

Mrs. Poggi: We'll have to use the credit card for the rest. Wait a minute . . . I think Gina has my credit card.

Mr. Poggi: You should get it back right away. You know Gina.

Mrs. Poggi: Yes, I do. And this morning she ran off to the mall to buy winter clothes.

Mr. Poggi: Winter? Why does she need winter clothes in Los Angeles?

Waiter: Excuse me, sir. Your credit card has been declined.

Mrs. Poggi: Uh-oh! Are you thinking what I'm thinking?

Pair On a piece of paper, make two lists. In the first, list the pros, or good things, about using a credit card. In the second, list the cons, or bad things. Compare the two lists. Is it a good idea to use a credit card?

1 Which bills have they paid?

Pair   Read the conversation again. Put a check (✓) next to the bills the Poggis have already paid. Then ask your partner the questions.

Examples:

Has Mr. Poggi **paid** for dinner yet?
   No, he **hasn't**.

Have the Poggis already **paid** the electric bill?
   Yes, they **have**.

_____ Dinner   _____ Insurance   _____ Alberto's tuition   _____ Gina's tuition   _____ Electric bill

2 A Family Budget

Listen to the Poggi family meeting. Then check if the statement is true, false, or you don't know.

	True	False	Don't Know
1. The Poggis haven't finished eating dinner.			
2. Alberto has studied for his test.			
3. The Poggis have decided to continue using the credit card.			
4. Alberto has saved a lot of money.			
5. Alberto has been good with money.			
6. Gina hasn't bought a lot of clothes.			
7. Gina has had a checking account in the past.			

3 What have they done?

Group   Listen to the tape again and discuss these questions.

1. What's the Poggis' problem?

2. What are they doing to solve their problem?

3. Do you agree with their solution? Can you think of other possible solutions?

   Mr. Poggi could _____

   Mrs. Poggi could _____

   Gina could _____

Did you know that . . . ?
In the United States, delinquent creditors are reported to a credit bureau. Lending institutions, like banks, usually get an applicant's credit history before approving a loan application.

4 Alberto has planned his budget.

Pair   Gina's brother, Alberto, has planned his budget very carefully. Look at Alberto's bulletin board and make sentences like those below.

Examples:

Alberto has decided to share an apartment with a roommate.

Alberto does not own a car.

What have you done to save money? In your notebook, write a paragraph about how you have saved money. Share any useful tips on saving money with your classmates.

5 Have you ever forgotten to pay a bill?

Group   Have one person in your group ask these questions and add up the score. Then compare your group's score with the other groups' scores. Which group has the best money managers?

1. _____ How many people in your group have forgotten to bring money to a restaurant?

2. _____ How many people in your group have forgotten to pay a bill?

3. _____ How many people in your group have had problems with a credit card?

4. _____ How many people in your group have lost money?

5. _____ How many people in your group have never budgeted their money?

   Total   _____

6 Information Gap Activity, pages 133 and 134.

Pair   Turn to pages 133 and 134 and follow your teacher's instructions.

7 Hear it. Say it.

The full forms are written below. Listen to the contracted forms and practice saying them.

Full forms and contractions with *have*

1. What have you done?
2. Who have they found?
3. When have I ever said that?
4. Why have we come?

5. Where have we heard that before?
6. How have you been?
7. What have you been up to?
8. How have they taken the news?

Pair Write your own questions. Ask your partner these questions using the contracted form.

1. Why have _____
2. Where have _____
3. What have _____
4. How have _____
5. When have _____

8 Have you ever made a budget?

To find out where your money goes, make a weekly budget. List all your expenses for a week. Then review your list and check (✓) whether each item is *optional* or *essential*.

Expenses	Optional	Essential

Pair Share your list with a partner. Discuss which optional expenses you can cut down on without cutting down on fun.

Lesson 2

In this lesson, you will

- open a checking account.
- call an account information line.
- record information in a check register.
- compare two monthly budgets.

I want to open a checking account.

Gina and her brother, Alberto, are opening checking accounts. Listen and read.

Gina Poggi
324 Green Lane
Riverside, CA 92501

1011

DATE *May 4, 2000*

PAY TO THE ORDER OF *Unica Card* $ *15.32*

Fifteen dollars and 32/100   DOLLARS

Memo *Monthly credit card payment*   *Gina Poggi*
Authorized Signature

⑈3110987⑈ ⑈0000249530⑈ 86

THE BANK **Checking**   DEPOSIT SLIP

Cash ▶ 25 00
Checks 69 00

CHECKING ACCOUNT NUMBER
★ 0000249530

Name *Gina Poggi*
Date: *May 21, 2000*
⑈3110987⑈

Total 94 00
Less Cash 15 00
Total $ 79.00

THE BANK **Checking**   WITHDRAWAL SLIP
Type of Account (Check One)
☑ Checking ☐ Savings ☐ Other

ACCOUNT NUMBER
★ 0000249530

Name *Gina Poggi*   Date: *May 21, 2000*
Amount (in words) *Fifty-four dollars*
Signature *Gina Poggi*
⑈3110987⑈   AMOUNT $ 54.00

Manager: Can I help you, miss?

Gina: Yes, we each want to open a checking account.

Manager: How many checks will you write every month?

Gina: Maybe ten to fifteen.

Manager: Then our Econo Checking Account is the one for you.

Gina: What kind of account is that?

Manager: There is no fee if you write fewer than twenty checks a month. You will also get an ATM card that you can use at ATM machines twenty-four hours a day to deposit money in your account or to get cash. You don't need to stand in line at the bank.

Gina: Great! Now I can go shopping at all hours of the day or night!

Alberto: Thank goodness the mall isn't open all night!

Pair Ask your partner: *Do you use an ATM card, or do you prefer to speak to a teller inside the bank? Why?*

1 Word Bag: At the Bank

Pair With your partner, write the number of each picture next to the correct word.

[ ] ATM card   [ ] check register   [ ] check   [ ] deposit slip

[ ] credit card [ ] bankbook   [ ] monthly statement [ ] withdrawal slip

2 Gina's Check Register

Pair Fill in Gina's check register. She wrote two checks this week: check #1010 to the Soap Shop on May 2 for $37.81, and check #1011 to the Unica Card on May 4 for $15.32.

ITEM NUMBER	DATE	CHECK OR DEPOSIT	ISSUED TO ISSUED FOR	T	CHECK OR DEBIT (—) AMOUNT	DEPOSIT OR CREDIT (—) AMOUNT	BLALNCE FWD.	
							850	00
1009	4/29	Acme Groceries			- $52.00		- 32 818	00
	5/1	Deposit				+ $300	+ 300 1,118	00
1010								
1011								
1012								
1013								
	5/15							

ITEM NUMBER	DATE	CHECK OR DEPOSIT	ISSUED TO ISSUED FOR	T	CHECK OR DEBIT (—) AMOUNT	DEPOSIT OR CREDIT (—) AMOUNT	BLALNCE FWD.

Gina wants to find out about her most recent transactions. She calls an account information line. Listen and fill in the register above.

3 Betty has a monthly budget, and Ann does too.

Pair   Compare Betty Poggi's budget with Ann Brennan's. In your opinion, who is a better money manager? Who has a more comfortable life?

Betty Poggi	
Monthly income	_$6,000_
Basic living expenses	
Phone	_$150_
Electric	_$95_
Insurance	_$250_
Food	_$750_
Clothing	_$900_
House payment	_$1100_
Cable TV	_$35_
Gas and car repair	_$100_
Entertainment	_$500_

Ann Brennan	
Monthly income	_$2,700_
Basic living expenses	
Phone	_$45_
Electric	_$100_
Insurance	_$300_
Food	_$350_
Clothing	_$200_
House payment	_$700_
Cable TV	_$25_
Gas and car repair	_$100_
Entertainment	_$50_

Using the information given above, write _T (true)_ or _F (false)_ before each sentence.

1. ____ Betty uses the phone a lot, and Ann does too.

2. ____ Ann spends a lot of money on entertainment, and Betty does too.

3. ____ Ann has bought a house, and Betty has too.

4. ____ Ann doesn't spend a lot of money on clothes, and Betty doesn't either.

5. ____ Betty is paying for insurance, and Ann is too.

Pair   In your notebook, write more sentences comparing Betty's and Ann's expenses. Write a paragraph comparing Ann's and Betty's monthly budgets.

4 Betty has a checking account, and Leonardo and Ann do too.

Look at the chart and complete the sentences.

	Betty	Leonardo	Ann	Jim
Checking account	✔	✔	✔	
Savings account	✔		✔	
ATM card	✔		✔	✔
Loan			✔	✔

1. Betty has a checking account, and _____Leonardo and Ann do too_____.

2. Leonardo isn't putting money in a savings account, and _____Jim isn't either_____.

3. Jim uses an ATM card, and _____.

4. Ann has opened a savings account, and _____.

5. Leonardo hasn't taken a loan, and _____.

In this lesson, you will

- interpret a pie chart.
- make a weekly food budget.
- listen to a radio broadcast for specific details.

Each dollar is a piece of your work.

What is "shopaholism"? Listen and read the magazine article to find out.

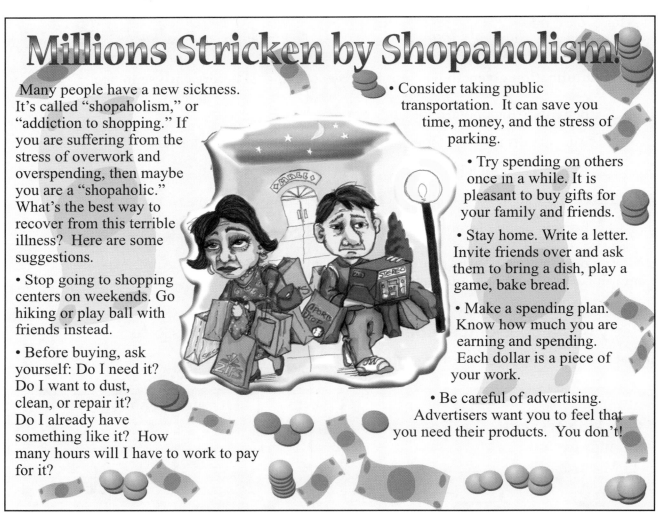

Millions Stricken by Shopaholism!

Many people have a new sickness. It's called "shopaholism," or "addiction to shopping." If you are suffering from the stress of overwork and overspending, then maybe you are a "shopaholic." What's the best way to recover from this terrible illness? Here are some suggestions.

• Stop going to shopping centers on weekends. Go hiking or play ball with friends instead.

• Before buying, ask yourself: Do I need it? Do I want to dust, clean, or repair it? Do I already have something like it? How many hours will I have to work to pay for it?

• Consider taking public transportation. It can save you time, money, and the stress of parking.

• Try spending on others once in a while. It is pleasant to buy gifts for your family and friends.

• Stay home. Write a letter. Invite friends over and ask them to bring a dish, play a game, bake bread.

• Make a spending plan. Know how much you are earning and spending. Each dollar is a piece of your work.

• Be careful of advertising. Advertisers want you to feel that you need their products. You don't!

Pair Discuss these questions with your partner.

1. Are you a "shopaholic"? How can you protect yourself from becoming one?

2. What necessary items do you buy frequently? What are some luxury items that you buy?

3. Do you ever have any money left after paying all your monthly bills? If so, what do you do with it?

1 Where does your money go?

How a Four-Person Family in the United States Spends Its Income

1 18% Food
2 18% Taxes
3 15% Housing
4 10% Electricity
5 9% Car payment
6 8% Gas
7 7% Shopping
    (clothing, appliances, etc.)
8 5% Life insurance
9 3% Entertainment (restaurants, movies, etc.)
10 3% Medical
11 2% Telephone
12 2% Car insurance

Median Income: $51,518
Data from U.S. Bureau of the Census

Group Calculate how much the average four-person family spends each month on:

1. Food _____

2. Taxes _____

3. Housing _____

4. Entertainment _____

5. Medical Expenses _____

Group How about in your country? Do a similar pie chart showing median income and spending habits of a four-person family in your country. Go to the library or use the Internet to get the information. Share your chart with the class.

Write a paragraph about what you do with any money left over after you pay all your bills.

2 Keep a check in your wallet.

Your checkbook can help you budget your money. Listen to the radio broadcast. Fill in the missing words.

- Keep a check in your wallet so you don't have to use your _____
- Put a clip on the _____ page you are working on so you always use the right _____.
- Write check numbers in the _____ ahead of time so you don't forget to record any checks you write.
- Use colored pens for different purposes (red for _____, blue for _____, green for _____) so you can easily see where your money goes.
- Carry a _____ so you always know exactly how much money is in your _____.
- Keep your checkbook _____ every month.

3 Online

Log onto **http://www.prenhall.com/brown_activities**
The Web: Balancing my budget
Grammar: What's your grammar IQ?
E-mail: I'm proud of myself!

4 Wrap Up

<u>Group</u> **Plan a weekly food budget for a family of four.**

1. Decide as a group how much you are going to spend on food for a week. Amount: _____

2. Check the items you want to buy from the list below. Write the name of the item, the number of items, and the price of each item on your shopping list. Be sure not to spend more money than your group has decided on. Share your list with the class. Discuss any problems you had in making the budget.

BAKERY
Bread __ Pie Crust __
Cake __ Cookies __
Other _____

DAIRY ITEMS
Butter __ Milk __
Eggs __ Spreads __
Other _____

FROZEN FOODS
Desserts __ Ice Cream __
Other _____

FRUIT
Apples __ Lemons __
Bananas __ Oranges __
Other _____

VEGETABLES
Onions __ Potatoes __
Lettuce __ Tomatoes __
Other _____

MEAT AND FISH
Bacon __ Pork __
Chicken __ Sausage __
Beef __ Steak __
Ham __ Shrimp __
Hot dogs __ Tuna __
Other _____

PAPER PRODUCTS
Napkins __ Paper
  towels __
Other _____

STAPLES
Catsup __ Rice __
Cereal __ Salt __
Coffee __ Soft drinks __
Flour __ Soups __
Juice __ Sugar __
Mustard __ Spices __
Oil __ Tea __
Other _____

Our Shopping List

Item	No. of items	Price
TOTAL		

Strategies for Success

➤ **Reading and reporting on a newspaper article**
➤ **Making lists**
➤ **Analyzing your motivation for learning English**

1. Find an English language newspaper and look at the financial/business pages or the sports pages. Take notes on an item of interest that has numbers in it. You and a partner report to each other about your article. Remember to ask questions.

2. From now on, make lists of "things to do" in English. Keep these lists where you will see them, and check things off when they are done. Doing this in English will be good practice for you.

3. Have you thought about why you're learning English? What motivates you? What can you do with your English skills? Write in your journal about (a) your reasons for learning English, (b) all the things you can read or listen to by knowing English, and (c) how English will help you in the future.

CHECKPOINT

How much have you learned in this unit? Review the goals for each lesson. What skills can you confidently use now? What skills do you need to practice? List these below.

Skills I've Learned Well

_____

_____

_____

_____

Skills I Need to Practice

_____

_____

_____

_____

Learning Preferences

In this unit, which type of activity did you like the best and the least? Write the number in the box: 1 = best; 2 = next best; 3 = next; 4 = least.

❑ Working by myself   ❑ Working with a group

❑ Working with a partner   ❑ Working as a whole class

In this unit, which exercises helped you to learn to:

listen more effectively?   Exercise _____   read more easily?   Exercise _____

speak more fluently?   Exercise _____   write more clearly?   Exercise _____

Which exercise did you like the most? _____   Why? _____

Which exercise did you like the least? _____   Why? _____

VOCABULARY

Verbs
budget
declined
deposit
enjoy
lose, lost
manage
record
relax

Nouns
bill
budget
bulletin board

cable TV
calculator
electricity
expenses
income
insurance
loan
mall
payment
pie chart
tuition
wallet

Adjectives
essential
extra
luxury
median
optional
wise

Expressions
bring a dish
Thank goodness!

Banking Terms
account
ATM card
balance
bankbook
check
checkbook
checking
  account
check register
credit card
deposit slip

interest
loan application
monthly
  statement
savings account
transaction
withdrawal slip

▶ GRAMMAR SUMMARY

Present Perfect Tense: Affirmative Statements

Subject	*Have/Has*	*(Already)*	Past Participle	Complement
I, You, We, They	have	(already)	studied	for the test.
He, She	has			

Contractions: I've, you've, he's, she's, we've, they've

Present Perfect Tense: Negative Statements

I (You, We, They) **haven't studied** for the test yet.
He (She) **hasn't studied** for the test yet.

Present Perfect Tense: *Have/Has* **Questions**   **Short Responses**

Have/Has	Subject	Past Participle	Complement	Short Response
Have	they	**studied**	for the test (yet)?	Yes, they have. No, they haven't.
Has	he/she	**studied**		Yes, he/she has. No, he/she hasn't.

Too/Either
Betty **uses** an ATM card, **and** Ann and Jim **do too**.
Alberto ***doesn't have*** a checking account, **and** Gina **doesn't have** one **either**.

▶ COMMUNICATION SUMMARY

Talking about budgets
We need to stop using credit cards.
We are going to write checks in the future.

Talking about actions that have already happened
I've written a check for the electric bill.
She's already bought clothes for the winter.

Opening a checking account
I want to open a checking account.
How many checks are you planning to write a month?

Comparing two monthly budgets
Ann doesn't spend a lot of money on clothes, and Betty doesn't either.
Betty is paying for insurance, and Ann is too.

Interpreting a pie chart
The average U.S. family spends about $770 a month on food.

Making a weekly food budget
We're going to spend $150 a week on food.

UNIT 9

Lesson 1

In this lesson, you will
- ask for and write a letter of recommendation.
- read employment ads.
- match skills and qualities with job requirements.

I'll be glad to give you a recommendation.

🎧 **Lynn is asking Mrs. Brennan for a letter of recommendation. Listen as you read.**

Mrs. Brennan: Why are you looking for a new job, Lynn? You were happy at your last job.

Lynn: I worked very hard. Do you remember when I was coming to class late? That was because of my job. I often got home at 11 P.M. I even stayed late because my co-worker didn't show up.

Mrs. Brennan: That was nice of you.

Lynn: My manager thanked me, and she said I was doing a great job. But she gave my co-worker a promotion!

Mrs. Brennan: You mean you were working because he didn't show up, and then he got the raise? Did you talk to your manager?

Lynn: Yes, but she said I didn't have enough experience. I think she had other reasons though, so I quit.

Mrs. Brennan: Would you like me to talk to her?

Lynn: No. I can get a better job. I just need a recommendation from someone who knows that I am a good worker.

Mrs. Brennan: I'll be glad to give you a recommendation, but you should let your manager's boss know why you are quitting.

Pair **Discuss these questions with your partner. Then share your ideas with the class.**

1. Do you agree with Mrs. Brennan's advice? If not, what advice would you give Lynn?

2. Have you ever had an experience like Lynn's in school or at work? If so, what did you do?

1 A Letter of Recommendation

Pair   Mrs. Brennan has written a letter of recommendation for Lynn. With a partner, fill in the blanks with the appropriate connector from the box.

when	because	before	but	so	and	after

March 23, 2000

To whom it may concern:

I am pleased to recommend Ms. Lynn Wang for the position of assistant to the Director of Human Resources. Ms. Wang has been my student at the World Language Center for the past year. She is friendly and well liked by classmates and teachers. She is very enthusiastic about her studies, _____ she is always willing to help her classmates. _____ she works
with other students, she listens to them carefully. In addition, her creative ideas make the class interesting.

_____ Lynn came to the World Language Center, very few people read the school newsletter. Now the newsletter is very popular _____ Lynn writes an interesting new column. _____ she graduates from the Language Institute, Lynn plans to study social work.

Ms. Wang is an outstanding candidate, _____ I recommend her highly for this position. You can contact me at 555-2384 if you have any questions, _____ please call between noon and 2:00 P.M.

Sincerely,

Ann Brennan

Associate Professor

Pair   Read the recommendation letter again.

1.   What are Lynn's good qualities?

_____   _____   _____

_____   _____   _____

2.   Your school is looking for an assistant at the Career Counselor's office. Who in your class would you recommend? _____

List this classmate's qualities: _____

Explain why you are recommending this person. _____

_____

2 Word Bag: Jobs

Pair   Write the name of the job under each picture.

disk jockey (DJ)   newscaster   graphic artist   social worker
tour guide   photojournalist   hair stylist   computer programmer
carpenter   civil engineer   veterinarian   flight attendant

1. _____   2. _____   3. _____   4. _____

5. _____   6. _____   7. _____   8. _____

9. _____   10. _____   11. _____   12. _____

3 Lynn should become a social worker because she likes to help people.

Pair   Look at the likes, abilities, and qualifications of the following people. With a partner, decide what job they should have and give a reason for your choice.

Robert could become a veterinarian **because** he likes animals.

Sandra can speak four languages, **so** she would be an excellent tour guide.

Likes, Abilities, and Qualifications

Masoud	Likes to construct model buildings	**Ana**	Likes animals
Alice	Can write interesting true stories	**David**	Likes to work with wood
Rosa	Likes to travel	**Jeff**	Has a pleasant speaking voice
Charles	Can solve word problems quickly	**Harry**	Loves to listen to popular music
Helen	Organizes soup kitchens and finds shelter for the homeless	**Leslie**	Has a new hairstyle every day

In your notebook, write sentences like those in the examples. Write about the likes, abilities, and qualifications of people you know. Share your sentences with the class.

4 A store manager should be friendly.

<u>Group</u>   Read the ads. With your group, decide which qualities are needed for each job. Write A, B, or C before each quality. (Some of the qualities are needed for more than one job.) Give reasons for your choices.

A. Store Manager
Family-run clothing store is looking for an individual with sales experience. We are especially interested in applicants who speak two or more languages. Mail résumé to 7215 Broadway, Riverside, CA 92501, or fax to 555-7968.

B. Security Officer
The Riverside Mall is accepting applications for two security officer positions. Applicants must have at least three years experience and a high-school diploma. Call 555-8791 for more info.

C. Social Worker
Looking for a social worker to become a member of our team. Candidates must have:
• Ability to handle several tasks at once
• Master's degree in social work
• Three years of experience
Contact Green Oaks Nursing and Rehabilitation Center at 555-6167 for more information.

Special Events Co-ordinator
Experienced creative person to plan

_____ outgoing

_____ creative

_____ sympathetic

_____ experienced with computers

_____ serious

_____ friendly

_____ patient

_____ organized

_____ bilingual

_____ funny

_____ physically strong

_____ team worker

_____ excellent attitude

_____ emotionally strong

_____ honest

Did you know that . . . ?
In the United States, students under eighteen years old need to get work permits from their schools in order to apply for part-time jobs.

5 Hear it. Say it.

Check the word you hear.

Minimal Pairs: /θ/ thank   /t/ tank

1. thank [ ]   tank [ ]
2. theme [ ]   team [ ]
3. thin [ ]   tin [ ]
4. thorn [ ]   torn [ ]

5. three [ ]   tree [ ]
6. threw [ ]   true [ ]
7. thick [ ]   tick [ ]
8. thigh [ ]   tie [ ]

<u>Pair</u>   With a partner, take turns pronouncing the pairs of words.

Lesson 2

In this lesson, you will
- discuss jobs you want.
- call about a job in an advertisement.

Careers for Multilinguals

🔊 **Would you like to work in international business? Listen as you read this article from the *ESL Newsletter*.**

ESL Newsletter

Summer 2001

Global Careers

As an ESL student, you may want to find a job in the global marketplace. You are not alone. Many learners of English and other languages are building successful careers all over the world. These days, the four most popular international careers are marketing, business administration, finance, and purchasing.

Marketing offers career opportunities in advertising, translating, and interpreting. Your knowledge of another culture and another language can be valuable to an international company.

People with business degrees who know several languages also have great opportunities. But if you want to work abroad, you should also know the requirements for working in another country.

If you study international laws for importing and exporting, you can open up new markets for products. If you are more interested in the product than the market, you might want to go into purchasing.

Many international students choose careers in finance. If you study different currencies and laws, you can find work as a treasurer or an international cash manager. Many companies need a knowledgeable multilingual employee to report on money invested in foreign banks.

If you can't decide which job you want, try continuing education classes. You may discover new skills and interests. In addition, career counselors can help you match your skills and language abilities with the right career. They can even help you contact the right companies. If you know two or more languages, the world may be yours.

by Lynn Wang

Pair Have you thought about your future career or job? If so, what is the job? Do you think learning English is important for your future career or job? Discuss.

1 I wanted to be an astronaut when I was a child.

Group Work in groups of three. Ask your group members about the jobs they were interested in when they were children, the kinds of jobs they want now, and the jobs they want in the future. Then add the information about yourself.

> What did you want to be when you were a child?
>
> What job do you want now?
>
> What is your dream job in the future?

Name	The Job I Wanted as a Child	The Job I Want/Have Now	My Dream Job
1.			
2.			
3. Myself			

Compare your answers with another group and discuss your reasons for choosing those jobs.

2 Help Wanted

Pair Read the employment ads. Then match the description with the job by writing *A*, *B*, or *C* in each blank.

A.

HELP WANTED
Typ. & filing. Exp. nec. Gd. bnfts. Excel. sal. Send resume to Box 41 DAILY NEWS.

B.

FILM LAB ASSISTANT
Work avail. for HS grads. Gd. hrs. Call for appt. from 9 to 5. 555-2356

C.

WAITERS/WAITRESSES
PT/FT work avail. now. Days & evenings $5.00/hr. plus tips. Call 555-6500

                                                        Job   Job

1. You have to type. _____   6. You can begin work today. _____

2. You can work full time or part time. _____   7. The salary is very good. _____

                                              8. You can't call to apply for this job. _____

3. You need previous experience. _____   9. You need to send a résumé. _____

4. You have to be a high school graduate. _____   10. You have to call during the day. _____

5. There are good benefits. _____   11. The job is in a restaurant. _____

Which job do you think Lynn is going to apply for? Which job would you apply for? Why?

3 How many years of experience do you have?

Listen to Lynn call about a job. Complete the notes.

Lynn's Notes

Salary: _____

Hours: _____

Benefits: _____

Interview: _____

Personnel Notes

Position: _____

Applicant's Name: ___*Lynn Wang*___

Applicant's years of experience: _____

Reason for wanting job: _____

Interview: _____

Pair   Do you think Lynn wants the job? How do you know?

4 Before you went to the interview, were you nervous?

Pair   Lynn is telling Pablo about her job interview. Choose the correct connector to complete the sentences.

Pablo: So, Lynn, _____ you went to the interview, were you nervous?
1. *before/after*

Lynn: I was a little nervous, _____ Mr. Johnson was very nice. I arrived early for the
2. *because/but*

   interview, _____ I made a list of questions to ask him.
   3. *so/because*

Pablo: What did you do _____ you couldn't answer a question?
4. *because/when*

Lynn: I just asked them to repeat the question, _____ I thought about it for a little
5. *and/but*

   while before answering.

Pablo: Do you think you got the job?

Lynn: I think I did _____ they asked me when I could start working. And Mr.
6. *because/so*

   Johnson introduced me to everyone _____ I left.
   7. *after/before*

In this lesson, you will
- identify parts of a résumé.
- write an employment ad.

Lynn's Résumé

Read Lynn's résumé.

Shieh Lin (Lynn) Wang
3657 Orange St.
Riverside, CA 92501
909-555-4576

Education

English Language Proficiency Certificate, World Language Center Riverside, CA	2000
High School Diploma, Xing Hua Academy, Beijing, China	1997

Work Experience

Internship at *China Daily News*. Beijing, China	1997

Extracurricular Activities

Features Editor, *ESL Newsletter*, Riverside, CA	1999
Student Volunteer, National Disaster Group, Riverside, CA	1998
Organizer, Students for a Better Community, Beijing, China	1995

Awards

First prize in essay writing competition, Beijing, China	1994
Student Leadership Awards, Xing Hua Academy, Beijing, China	1995

Memberships

Student Editors Guild, World Language Institute
Member of the Honors Society, Xing Hua Academy, Beijing, China

References

Available upon request.

Pair Read Lynn's résumé again. Discuss it with your partner. Is it a good résumé? Is any information missing? Does the résumé give you a picture of Lynn as a worker and student? Share your opinion with the class.

1 When you apply for a job, you should have a résumé.

🔊 **Listen as you read the résumé-writing tips below.**

> Many employers ask you to send a résumé before they decide to interview you. Your résumé helps them form a first impression of you, so make sure your résumé is good! Check your spelling, grammar, and punctuation. Make sure your résumé is well organized and easy to read. A résumé should include:
>
> 1. **Personal information:** your name, address, and telephone number
> 2. **Education:** where and when you went to school, and what you studied
> 3. **Employment experience:** the jobs you have had in the past
> 4. **References:** people who know you well
>
> In addition, you can include a career goal (what kind of job you want to get), any languages you speak, special skills, other activities and memberships, and awards or honors.

Pair Match each piece of information to the correct part of the résumé.

❶ Award for outstanding achievement in computer science, 1997, Eastview High School
Best Salesperson of the Year, 1998, Computech

❷ Claire Peritz
Manager, Computech
914-555-4646

❸ 1997–1999 Assistant Manager
Computech, Hartsdale, NY

❹ An entry-level job in marketing, with opportunity for growth

❺ Knowledge of computer programming languages
Fluent in Spanish, English, and Portuguese

❻ Bernardo Díaz
223 East 10th Street
New York, NY 10010
212-555-3892

❼ Member, Computer Retailers Association
Volunteer, Big Brothers of America, Westchester County, NY

❽ 1997 High School Diploma
Eastview High School, Eastview, NY

_8_ Education
____ Work Experience
____ Skills
____ Extracurricular Activities and Memberships
____ Personal Information
____ Honors and Awards
____ Career Goal
____ References

List your skills in your notebook. What type of job can you apply for with your current skills?

Pair Share your list with your partner. Discuss jobs that each of you can possibly apply for.

2 Information Gap Activity, pages 135 and 136.

Pair   Turn to pages 135 and 136 and follow your teacher's instructions.

3 Online

Log onto **http://www.prenhall.com/brown_activities**
The Web: Looking for a job
Grammar: What's your grammar IQ?
E-mail: Job experiences

4 Wrap Up

Group   Your school is going to hire a new English teacher. Write an ad for the position. Include all the qualifications you're looking for in the applicants. Look at the ads on page 100. You may want to use some of the qualities from that exercise in your ad.

Compare your ad with another group's and be prepared to discuss your reasons for the qualifications you seek in the applicants.

Strategies for Success

➤ **Planning interview questions and role playing an interview**
➤ **Revising your writing**
➤ **Reviewing vocabulary items**

1. In the classified ad section in an English-language newspaper, look up "jobs" or "help wanted" ads. Look for jobs that you could qualify for with your present English ability and your experience. With a partner, plan a set of interview questions that you can ask each other, then role play an interview for some of the jobs you found.

2. In your workbook, you wrote an application letter. With a partner, read each other's letters and offer advice on how to make the letters better. Look at the models in your workbook.

3. This unit has lots of new vocabulary. Review the vocabulary on your own by making a sentence with each word. Then, with a partner, quiz each other.

CHECKPOINT

How much have you learned in this unit? Review the goals for each lesson. What skills can you confidently use now? What skills do you need to practice? List these below.

Skills I've Learned Well

_____

_____

_____

_____

Skills I Need to Practice

_____

_____

_____

_____

Learning Preferences

In this unit, which type of activity did you like the best and the least? Write the number in the box: 1 = best; 2 = next best; 3 = next; 4 = least.

❑ Working by myself   ❑ Working with a group

❑ Working with a partner   ❑ Working as a whole class

In this unit, which exercises helped you to learn to:

listen more effectively?   Exercise _____   read more easily?   Exercise _____

speak more fluently?   Exercise _____   write more clearly?   Exercise _____

Which exercise did you like the most? _____   Why? _____

Which exercise did you like the least? _____   Why? _____

VOCABULARY

Verbs
accept
contact
offer
qualify
quit
recommend
type

Adjectives
bilingual
creative
enthusiastic
entry-level
friendly
hard-working
honest
multilingual
organized
outgoing
outstanding
patient
sympathetic
unfair

Nouns
awards
business
  administration
career
extracurricular
  activities
finance
individual
letter of
  recommendation
marketing
opportunity
promotion
purchasing
reference
résumé
volunteer

Occupations
carpenter
civil engineer
computer
  programmer
disk jockey
flight attendant
graphic artist
hair stylist
newscaster
photojournalist
security officer
social worker
tour guide
veterinarian

► GRAMMAR SUMMARY

Complex Sentences

Independent clause	Dependent clause	
	Connector	Rest of clause
She wrote a résumé	**before**	she applied for the job.
He got an entry-level job	**after**	he finished college.
I wanted to be an astronaut	**when**	I was a child.
Lynn should become a social worker	**because**	she likes to help people.

Dependent clause		Independent clause
Linking word	Rest of clause	
When	I was a child	I wanted to be a hair stylist.
Before	Lynn went to the interview	she was nervous.

► COMMUNICATION SUMMARY

Asking for a letter of recommendation
Would you please write a letter of recommendation for me?
I was wondering if you could write me a letter of recommendation?

Writing a letter of recommendation
I am pleased to recommend Ms. Lynn Wang for the position.
She is friendly and well liked by her classmates and teachers.

Matching skills and qualities with job requirements
Lynn should become a social worker because she likes to help people.
A social worker should be patient and friendly.

Discussing jobs you want
I want to get an entry-level job in marketing.

Calling about an advertised job
Hello, my name is Lynn Wang.
I'm calling about the job that was advertised in the newspaper yesterday.

Identifying parts of a résumé
Career Goal: An entry-level job in marketing, with opportunity for growth
Skills: Fluent in Spanish, English, and Portuguese

Writing an employment ad
Looking for a social worker to work with our team.
We are especially interested in candidates who speak two or more languages.

Lesson 1

In this lesson, you will
- talk about predictions.
- make promises.

Something wonderful will happen soon.

🔊 **Do you ever wonder what will happen to your friends in the future? Read and listen to the conversation.**

Yumiko: I think Yon Mi is going back to Korea very soon.

Nelson: Me too. She seems sad lately. She got another letter from her boyfriend. Maybe he's going to marry someone else.

Yumiko: I think she is just very homesick.

Gina: All of us are a little homesick. But she also has to make a very big decision. If she makes the wrong decision, she'll regret it.

Yumiko: Yeah, I'm glad I'm not in her shoes.

Nelson: But everybody has to deal with problems like hers sometime.

Gina: I'll talk to her. I just know everything will work out. Maybe I can help her.

Gina: You're worried about something, aren't you?

Yon Mi: Yes, I am.

Gina: Making important decisions can be very difficult.

Yon Mi: That's right. I wonder what's going to happen to me?

Gina: Don't worry. If you're patient, something wonderful will happen soon.

Yon Mi: How can you be sure?

Gina: You're intelligent and caring. You won't be unhappy forever. You have to wait and see, but someday soon you'll be happy.

Pair **With your partner, talk about why Gina is sure that Yon Mi will be happy soon.**

1 Ahmed will get a part-time job.

Mixer   Talk to four classmates about their plans for the future. What will happen to them in the near future? Use *will* + verb to write a prediction for each person.

Examples:

Sachiko **will move** to Tokyo.

Ahmed **will get** a part-time job.

1. _____

2. _____

3. _____

4. _____

2 Will Yon Mi marry Han?

Pair   What will happen to Yon Mi? Gina thinks she knows. What does Lynn ask?

Will	Subject	Main Verb	
Will	I, we you he, she, it they	**be**	here on time?

1. Yon Mi / marry Han

    Lynn: <u>Will Yon Mi marry Han?</u>
    Gina: Yes, I think she will.

2. they / be happy

    Lynn: _____
    Gina: Yes, they will.

3. they / live in California

    Lynn: _____
    Gina: No, they won't.

4. Yon Mi / quit her studies

    Lynn: _____
    Gina: No, I don't think she will.

5. Han / be a good father

    Lynn: _____
    Gina: Yes, I think he will.

3 I'll do anything for you!

Pair   You're going to marry someone you love very much. What will you promise him or her to do after you get married? Complete the following sentences with *will* (*'ll*) or *will not* (*won't*). Then create a sentence of your own. Compare your answers with a partner.

Pronoun + *will*	Affirmative Contraction	Negative Contraction
I **will**	I'll	I **won't**
You **will**	You'll	You **won't**
He, She, It **will**	He'll, She'll, It'll	He, She, It **won't**
We, They **will**	We'll, They'll	We, They **won't**

1.   I _____ always be there for you.

2.   You _____ never be unhappy.

3.   We _____ share the house chores.

4.   I _____ bring home my work.

5.   I _____ complain about every little thing.

6.   We _____ take a vacation every year.

7.   I _____ forget your birthday.

8.   _____

4 Predictions

Pair   Ask a question about each prediction below. Then compare your questions with your partner. What kinds of answers would you like to hear? Share with the class.

Prediction: Your life will change soon.

1.   You will take an important trip.

2.   You will change your career plans.

Question: Will it **affect** my family?

3.   You will meet someone special.

4.   One of your dreams will come true.

5 Hear it. Say it.

Listen to the following sentences and practice pronouncing them.

Contractions with *will*

1.   We'll see about it later.

2.   What'll you have?

3.   That'll come later.

4.   There'll be more to do.

5.   I'll let you know.

6.   It'll be a surprise.

Pair   Complete the sentences using your own words. Then practice pronouncing them.

1.   We'll _____

2.   There'll _____

3.   They'll _____

4.   I'll _____

5.   It'll _____

6.   You'll _____

6 What will happen next?

Pair   What will happen next in each situation? Write your predictions. Then compare them with the predictions of another pair.

1.   <u>The mother will take the child away from the pool. She'll watch the child more carefully.</u>

2.   _____

3.   _____

4.   _____

5.   _____

6.   _____

7 Optimist or Pessimist?

An optimist looks at the bright side and thinks everything will turn out well in the future. A pessimist is gloomy and sees only unhappiness in the future. Listen to the following predictions. For each prediction, write *optimist* or *pessimist*.

1.   _____   2. _____   3. _____

What do you think the world will be like in the year 2100? In your notebook, make a list of your predictions. Then write a paragraph about your predictions. Exchange paragraphs with a partner. Is your partner an optimist or a pessimist?

Lesson 2

In this lesson, you will
- talk about future goals.
- talk about future possibilities.

What will you do if you have the time?

Do you like surprises? Read and listen to the conversation.

Oscar: Gosh, the semester was short. Are any of you going to come back next semester?

Gina: Not me. I'm going to UCLA!

Yumiko: Will you take English classes there?

Gina: I don't know yet.

Lynn: I'm going to work this summer in a film lab.

Pablo: Maybe you'll meet movie stars there!

Lynn: With my luck, if I meet a movie star, it will probably be Count Dracula!

Pablo: Well, I'm going to keep studying English. If I have the time, I'll learn a water sport.

Yumiko: I haven't decided yet. If I have enough money, I'll visit my aunt in New York. But the airfare is very expensive.

Ivan: I don't have any definite plans either. What are your plans, Yon Mi?

Yon Mi: Well, you all seem very sure about your lives. I'm not sure about mine. Last night I couldn't sleep. I called my mother in Korea. If I go home, my mother will be very happy. I tried to call Han, but he didn't answer the phone. I didn't know what to do. So, I lay awake thinking and wondering. What is my future? What kind of person will I be? Finally, I decided to . . . oh my goodness . . . Is that you, Han?!

Pair   Why do you think Han has decided to visit Yon Mi in Riverside? What do you think will happen? Share your opinions with the class.

1 His plans are definite, but hers aren't.

__Pair__   Write sentences using the subjects given for each item below.

1. Pablo; Gina
   <u>His plans are definite, but hers aren't.</u>

2. I; you
   _____

3. Lynn and Pablo; Ivan and you
   _____

4. Yumiko; I
   _____

5. We; Gina and Yon Mi
   _____

6. Lynn; Nelson
   _____

Subject Pronoun	Possessive Adjective	Possessive Pronoun
I	my	mine
you	your	yours
he	his	his
she	her	hers
we	our	ours
they	their	theirs

Did you know that . . . ?
In the United States, interracial marriages are widely accepted. Also, parents rarely "arrange" a marriage for their child.

2 Word Bag: Future Plans

__Pair__   Write the name of the activity under each picture.

get a job / an internship   go back home   hang out with my friends
keep taking English classes   travel   take some time off

1. _____   2. _____   3. _____

4. _____   5. _____   6. _____

__Group__   Ask your group members: *What are you going to do after this semester? Do your plans depend on other things?* Take notes and report to the class.

Example:

A: What are you going to do after this semester?
B: Well, **if I pass this course, I'll transfer** to State University.

3 What will happen if . . .

Read these sentences about love and marriage. Complete the sentences on your own.

Examples:

Han **will marry** another person if Yon Mi **doesn't return** to Korea.

If Yon Mi **doesn't** return to Korea, Han **will marry** another person.

1. <u>Her fiancé will be very unhappy</u> if Yon Mi decides to finish her studies in the United States.

2. _____ if she breaks up with her fiancé.

3. _____ if her fiancé decides to come to the United States.

4. _____ if she decides to go back to Korea.

What about you?

5. If I marry someone from a different country, _____.

6. If I marry someone from my country, _____.

7. If I never marry anyone, _____.

Pair **Compare your completed sentences with your partner's sentences.**

4 What will my family think?

Pair **If you marry someone from a different country, what will your family members say? Answer the questions below. Then share your answers with your partner.**

1. What will your mother or father say? _____

2. your brothers and sisters? _____

3. your friends? _____

Write a paragraph about what people will say and do if you marry a person from another country.

Lesson 3

In this lesson, you will
- talk about future goals and plans.
- share memories.

What will you remember them for?

Mrs. Brennan's students have created a yearbook. Read and listen to what they say about their classmates.

Nelson Balewa
thoughtful, helpful

Favorite question:
  "How?"

Will be remembered for:
  Solving problems

Ambition:
  To be a scientist

Pablo Bonilla
cheerful, intelligent

Favorite question:
  "Why don't we . . . ?"

Will be remembered for:
  The piñata caper

Ambition:
  To be a pilot

Gina Poggi
beautiful, friendly

Favorite question:
  "What if?"

Will be remembered for:
  Shopping and credit cards

Ambition:
  To be a fashion designer

Tony Silva
traditional, patient, careful

Favorite question:
  "What?"

Will be remembered for:
  His attention to detail

Ambition:
  To be a doctor

Yon Mi Lee
shy, gentle, strong

Favorite question:
  "Should we . . . ?"

Will be remembered for:
  Her smile

Ambition:
  To be an opera singer

Lynn Wang
creative, caring, understanding

Favorite question:
  "Why?"

Will be remembered for:
  Telling good stories

Ambition:
  To be an author

Pair Ask each other these questions: *Which of Mrs. Brennan's students is your favorite? Why?* Share your opinion with the class.

1 Make a prediction.

Pair How well do you know the students in this book? With your partner, choose four of the students and make a prediction about each one's future. Then compare your predictions with another pair.

Example:

<u>Lynn</u> : <u>She'll be a social worker because she is an understanding and caring person</u> .

Ivan Nelson Gina Yumiko Yon Mi Pablo Tony Oscar

1. _____ : _____ .
2. _____ : _____ .
3. _____ : _____ .
4. _____ : _____ .

Choose one of the four. In your notebook, write a paragraph about the future of this person. Do you think this person will realize his or her ambition? Why or why not?

2 What are you going to do?

Group Work in a group of three. Ask your group about their future plans. Add one more question. Then report your group's future plans to the class.

Example: All of us are **going to go** back to our native countries during the break.

Questions	Name	Name	Name
1. What are you going to do during the semester break?			
2. What is your plan for next semester?			
3. What do you plan to do after you finish your English studies?			
4.			

3 Information Gap Activity, pages 137 and 138.

Pair Turn to pages 137 and 138 and follow your teacher's instructions.

4 Online

Log onto **http://www.prenhall.com/brown_activities**
The Web: Words of wisdom
Grammar: What's your grammar IQ?
E-mail: My hopes and dreams

5 Wrap Up

<u>Group</u>   Every culture has traditional superstitions. Look at these superstitions. Discuss what each means. Is it supposed to bring good luck or bad luck? Why do you think so?

If you break a mirror, you'll have seven years of bad luck.

<u>Class</u>   Does your country have any superstitions? Share them with the class.

<u>Pair</u>   Make two lists. In the first list, give reasons why people believe in superstitions. In the second list, give reasons why people do not believe in superstitions. Then write one paragraph, using each list.

Finally, write whether you believe in any superstitions and give your reasons. Share your paragraph with the class.

Strategies for Success

➤ Writing about your future
➤ Reviewing and analyzing goals you have set
➤ Discussing goals with classmates

1. In your journal, write about your future hopes and dreams. Try to be as detailed as possible about your future.

2. Look back at the goals you set in Unit 1 and reviewed and revised in Unit 5. In your journal, record (a) those you achieved completely, (b) those you did not achieve yet, and (c) those you achieved partially. Make a new list of goals for your English learning after this course in English.

3. With a partner, or in groups of three or four, talk about the goals you completed and those you are still working on. The other people might give you some good ideas of goals you could make for yourself.

CHECKPOINT

How much have you learned in this unit? Review the goals for each lesson. What skills can you confidently use now? What skills do you need to practice? List these below.

Skills I've Learned Well

_____

_____

_____

_____

Skills I Need to Practice

_____

_____

_____

_____

Learning Preferences

In this unit, which type of activity did you like the best and the least? Write the number in the box: 1 = best; 2 = next best; 3 = next; 4 = least.

❑ Working by myself   ❑ Working with a group

❑ Working with a partner   ❑ Working as a whole class

In this unit, which exercises helped you to learn to:

listen more effectively?   Exercise _____   read more easily?   Exercise _____

speak more fluently?   Exercise _____   write more clearly? Exercise _____

Which exercise did you like the most? _____   Why? _____

Which exercise did you like the least? _____   Why? _____

VOCABULARY

Verbs	Nouns	Adjectives	Expressions
change	airfare	afraid	be able to
complain	caper	awake	be in someone's
get	fiancé	caring	shoes
go back	film	definite	break up with
happen	household	interracial	hang out
lie, lay, lain	chores	patient	someday soon
predict	internship	sure	someone special
promise	major	wonderful	take some time off
regret	optimist	worried	with my luck
share	pessimist		work out
transfer	semester		
visit	superstition		
wonder			

► GRAMMAR SUMMARY

Simple Future: *Will*

Subject	*Will*	Verb	Complement
I, You, We, They, He, She	**will**	**take**	an important trip.

Simple Future: *Will (Yes/No* Question)

Will	Subject	Verb	Complement
Will	you	**share**	the chores?

Short Response

Yes, I will. *or* No, I won't.

Real Conditional

If-Clause (Simple Present)	Independent or Main Clause (Future)
If I need money,	**I will get** a job.

Independent or Main Clause (Future)	*If*-Clause (Simple Present)
I will get a job	**if I need** money.

Possessive Pronouns

Subject Pronoun	Possessive Adjective	Possessive Pronoun
I	my	mine
you	your	yours
he	his	his
she	her	hers
we	our	ours
they	their	theirs

► COMMUNICATION SUMMARY

Talking about predictions
Sachiko will move to Tokyo.

Making promises
I'll always love you.
I won't forget to call you.

Talking about future possibilities
If she finds a new job, she will move to a bigger house.
If I have money, I'll visit my aunt in New York.

Talking about future plans and goals
I'm going to finish my studies and open my own business.
We're going to visit you in Japan next summer.

Sharing memories
I'll remember our evenings at the coffee shop.

▶ GAMES AND ACTIVITIES

Communication Activity   **Group 1**

Don't get up at 5 A.M.	Don't eat out every night	Can swim	Speak more than two languages	Can't dance the tango
_____		_____	_____	_____
Can say "Good-bye" in five languages	Don't jog	Can tell a joke in English	Play the guitar	Are living with your family
_____	_____	_____	_____	_____
Go shopping every week	Can whistle	Are taking a vacation this year	Don't wear a uniform	Don't play soccer
_____	_____	_____	_____	_____

Unit 1 Blackline Master 121

Can't bake a cake	Can stand on your head	Like pizza	Aren't planning a trip to Alaska	Drink black coffee
_____	_____	_____	_____	_____
Aren't studying Japanese	Don't have a pet	Haven't met a movie star	Write in a journal	Have brothers or sisters
_____	_____	_____	_____	_____
Can eat with chopsticks	Can use a computer	Eat a big breakfast	Take a cold shower before breakfast	Don't own a bicycle
_____	_____	_____	_____	_____

Read the information in your chart. Ask your partner questions to fill in the missing information in your chart. Don't look at your partner's page!

Early Explorers

Name and Nationality	Start of Journey (Where and When)		Place Visited and When Visited		Adventure Encountered	How Journey Ended
	Year	Town	Place	Year		
Leif Ericsson Norse			Norway Vinland	1000 1001	Rescued sailors from a wrecked ship	
Christopher Columbus Italian	1492	Genoa	San Salvador Hispanola		Fought battles with "Indians" (Native Americans)	Returned home (1496)
Genghis Khan Mongolian	1206	Karakorum				Returned home (1225)
Marco Polo Italian			Middle East China			Returned home (1295)

Useful Language

Where did he live?

When did he start his journey?

What places did he visit?

When did he visit _____?

What adventures did he have?

When did he return home?

Information Gap Activity

Read the information in your chart. Ask your partner questions to fill in the missing information in your chart. Don't look at your partner's page!

Early Explorers

Name and Nationality	Start of Journey (Where and When)		Place Visited and When Visited		Adventure Encountered	How Journey Ended
	Year	Town	Place	Year		
Leif Ericsson Norse	999	Brattahild				Returned home (1005)
Christopher Columbus Italian				1492 1493		
Genghis Khan Mongolian			Asia Middle East	1213 1219	Took control of many countries	
Marco Polo Italian	1271	Venice		1271 1275	Escorted a Mongol princess	

Useful Language

Where did he live?

When did he start his journey?

What places did he visit?

When did he visit _____?

What adventures did he have?

When did he return home?

Information Gap Activity Student A

You and your partner are investigating a burglary at the City Bistro. You have already interviewed some of the suspects to find out what they were doing when the robbery took place. On the left below are your notes of your interview with the suspects. Ask your partner questions to find out what the suspects listed on the right side of the page were doing when the robbery took place. Don't look at your partner's page!

Suspect	What each was doing at the time
Mark	having dinner at Bill's house
Teresa	studying at home
Jimisu	having dinner with Bob
Harry	visiting his girlfriend Mary
Don	having coffee in the City Bistro

Suspect	What each was doing at the time
Susan	
Bill	
John	
Bob	
Mary	

Who was the burglar?

Useful Language

What was (*name*) doing when the robbery took place?
He or She was _____ing.

This morning these students were all late for class. You know why some of these students were late. Ask your partner questions to find out why the other students were late. Write the reasons in the chart below. Don't look at your partner's page!

Ana	Overslept.	**Irene**	
Bai	Alarm clock didn't ring.	**Jay**	
Cathy		**Kay**	Forgot her wallet.
Don		**Lem**	Car ran out of gas.
Elena	Missed the bus.	**Maria**	

Useful Language

Why was (*name*) late?
Because_____.

Information Gap Activity Student B

You and your partner are investigating a burglary at the City Bistro. You have already interviewed some of the suspects to find out what they were doing when the robbery took place. On the left below are your notes of your interview with the suspects. Ask your partner questions to find out what the suspects listed on the right of the page were doing when the robbery took place. Don't look at your partner's page!

Suspect	What each was doing at the time
Susan	studying at Teresa's house
Bill	having dinner with Mark
John	having coffee with Don
Bob	in a restaurant with Jimisu
Mary	watching TV alone

Suspect	What each was doing at the time
Mark	
Teresa	
Jimisu	
Harry	
Don	

Who was the burglar?

Useful Language

**What was (*name*) doing when the robbery took place?
He or She was _____ing.**

This morning these students were all late for class. You know why some of these students were late. Ask your partner questions to find out why the other students were late. Write the reasons in the chart below. Don't look at your partner's page!

Ana	
Bai	
Cathy	Had a headache.
Don	Drove his father to work.
Elena	

Irene	Sprained her ankle.
Jay	Forgot his books.
Kay	
Lem	
Maria	Thought it was Saturday.

Useful Language

**Why was (*name*) late?
Because _____.**

Information Gap Activity Student A

Look at the quiz below. Make sure your partner doesn't see the information on the right of your questionnaire. Read the questions on the left and the information on the right. With the information that you have, answer each question by yourself. When you and your partner have finished, review each other's information and compare your answers. Who has the most correct answers?

1. **Which structure is taller?** a. the Empire State Building b. the Eiffel Tower	The Eiffel Tower: 984.5 feet
2. **Which animal is heavier?** a. The elephant b. The hippopotamus	The elephant: 12,000 pounds
3. **Which university is older?** a. Harvard b. Yale	Yale: founded 1700
4. **Which is the faster animal?** a. The elephant b. The cheetah	The elephant: 25 m.p.h.
5. **Which U.S. professionals have a larger vocabulary?** a. Lawyers b. Journalists	Journalists: 20,000 words
6. **Which continent's population is larger?** a. Africa b. Asia	Asia: 2.82 billion
7. **Which city's population is larger?** a. Mexico City b. Cairo	Cairo: 10 million people

Look at the quiz below. Make sure your partner doesn't see the information on the right of your questionnaire. Read the questions on the left and the information on the right. With the information that you have, answer each question by yourself. When you and your partner have finished, review each other's information and compare your answers. Who has the most correct answers?

1. **Which Structure is taller?**
  a. the Empire State Building
  b. the Eiffel Tower
	The Empire State Building: 1,250 feet

2. **Which animal is heavier?**
  a. The elephant
  b. The hippopotamus
	The hippopotamus: 8,000 pounds

3. **Which university is older?**
  a. Harvard
  b. Yale
	Harvard: founded 1636

4. **Which is the faster animal?**
  a. The elephant
  b. The cheetah
	The cheetah: 70 m.p.h.

5. **Which U.S. professionals have a larger vocabulary?**
  a. Lawyers
  b. Journalists
	Lawyers: 15,000 words

6. **Which continent's population is larger?**
  a. Africa
  b. Asia
	Africa: 0.56 billion

7. **Which city's population is larger?**
  a. Mexico City
  b. Cairo
	Mexico City: 22 million

You and your partner are having lunch at the Riverside Oaks Restaurant. You are watching your weight. Your partner's menu has calorie information; yours has only the prices. First, check (✓) the items you want to order. Then find out if your order is within your calorie limit by asking your partner for the calorie counts of the items you have chosen. Take notes. Change your order if there are too many calories in your lunch. Look at the Calorie Chart below to see how many calories you should have. Don't look at your partner's page!

CALORIE CHART FOR LUNCH

	Women	Men
To maintain weight:	650 calories	900 calories
To lose weight:	less than 650 calories	less than 900 calories
To gain weight:	more than 650 calories	more than 900 calories

If you are watching your weight, consult the list for

CALORIES IN TODAY'S MENU

Main Courses ◆

Roast chicken	$4.50
Steak	$6.75
Broiled whitefish	$7.75

Vegetables ◆

Rice	$.85
French fries	$.85
Peas	$.60
Carrots	$.60

Salads ◆

Tomato	$1.95
Caesar	$2.50
Bread and butter	$.50

Desserts ◆

Cheesecake	$1.50
Chocolate cake	$1.75
Fresh fruit	$1.10

Drinks ◆

Beer	$3.00
Wine	$3.50
Orange Juice	$1.10
Tea	$.65
(with or without sugar and milk)	
Coffee	$.95
(with or without sugar and cream)	

Useful Language

How many calories are there in the _roast chicken_?
How about in the _French fries_?
It's $3.50. or $3.50.

You and your partner are having lunch at the Riverside Oaks Restaurant. You are watching your diet as well as your budget. You don't want to spend more than $10 for your lunch. Use the menu to order a lunch within your budget and your calorie limit. Check (✓) the items you want. Then ask your partner the cost of each of these items. Change your order to stay within your budget and within your calorie limit. Don't look at your partner's page!

CALORIE CHART FOR LUNCH

	Women	Men
To maintain weight:	650 calories	900 calories
To lose weight:	less than 650 calories	less than 900 calories
To gain weight:	more than 650 calories	more than 900 calories

If you are watching your weight, consult the list for

CALORIES IN TODAY'S MENU

Main Courses

Roast chicken	225 cal.
Steak	585 cal.
Broiled whitefish	150 cal.

Vegetables

Rice	260 cal.
French fries	450 cal.
Peas	55 cal.
Carrots	40 cal.

Salads

Tomato	120 cal.
Caesar	190 cal.
Bread	65 cal.
with butter	100 cal.

Desserts

Cheesecake	320 cal.
Chocolate cake	470 cal.
Fresh fruit	115 cal.

Drinks

Beer	180 cal.
Wine	100 cal.
Orange Juice	140 cal.
Tea, plain	5 cal.
with milk	15 cal.
with sugar	40 cal.
with milk and sugar	60 cal.
Coffee, plain	5 cal.
with cream	25 cal.
with sugar	40 cal.
with cream and sugar	70 cal.

Useful Language

How much is *roast chicken*?
How about a *Caesar salad*? How much is it?
There are *225 calories* in the *roast chicken*. or *225* calories.

Information Gap Activity

You are a telephone salesperson for the Best Wear Company. Your partner is a customer. Your partner calls to order some items from your company's catalog. Take the order and fill out the order form. Make sure you have written the order correctly by asking your partner to confirm it. Don't look at your partner's page!

Ordered by:

Name _____

Address _____

City _____

State _____ Zip _____

Telephone _____

Ship to: (Use only if different from "ORDERED BY")

Name _____

Address _____

City _____

State _____ Zip _____

Item number	Quantity	Color	Size	Description	Unit price	Total

Check Method of Payment:

( ) check / money order   ( ) VISA   ( ) MASTERCARD

Card number: _____

Expiration date: _____

Merchandise Total	
Shipping and Handling	
Total	

Useful Language

Answering the telephone:	Hello, Best Wear Company.
Asking for information:	What's the item number (or price)?
	What color (or size) would you like?
Confirming the order:	Did you say the item number (or price or color or size) was . . .?
Ending the conversation:	Thank you for your order. Good-bye.

You want to place a catalog order. Your partner is a telephone salesperson. Look at the catalog page below. Choose two items you want to buy. Call the Best Wear Company and give your order to your partner. Make sure that your partner takes the order correctly by confirming the information. Don't look at your partner's page!

40% OFF ALL SLEEPWEAR FOR BOYS

#1234X BOYS' FLANNEL PAJAMAS
Sizes: S, M, L, XL.
Colors: Red, Blue, Green
Reg. $20, **Sale** $11.99

SAVE ON GIRLS' JEANS
$9.99

#0017G GIRLS' HIGH MOUNTAIN JEANS
Slim & Regular Sizes 7–16.
Colors: Blue, Brown, Black
Reg. $15, **Sale** $9.99

SAVE ON GIFTS FOR MEN

$14.95

#1185D CLASSIC SUEDE SLIPPERS
Sizes: 7/8–12/13.
Reg. $20, **Sale** $14.95

ALL WATCHES ARE ON SALE!
$29.99 *each*

WATER-RESISTANT SPORTS WATCHES
SHOWN:
A. # 7875P EXPLORER
B. # 7876Q GOLDMAN
C. # 7877F DECATHLON
Reg. $39.99, **Sale** $29.99

EVERY SWEATER FOR HER IS ON SALE!

$17.99

#2323W COTTON/ACRYLIC SWEATERS
Sizes: S, M, L.
Colors: Black, Red, Green, Blue
Reg. $28, **Sale** $17.99

25%–40% OFF ALL WOMENS' HANDBAGS!

A. #4440H VINYL TOTE
Black only. Reg. $14, **Sale** $10.99
B. #4445B PATCHED LEATHER BAG
Colors: Black, Brown.
Reg. $24.99, **Sale** $19.99
C. #4447B DENIM BACKPACK
Blue only. Reg. $20, **Sale** $14.99

Useful Language

Starting the conversation:	**Hello. I'd like to place an order.**
Placing an order:	**I'd like . . . .**
Confirming the order:	**Yes, I said the item number (price or color or size) is . . . .**

Gina, Lynn, Tony, and Pablo are doing their housework. Each has made a list of chores to do. You have the lists for Gina and Tony; your partner has the lists for Lynn and Pablo. Ask each other questions to find out who has finished which chores. In your lists, check (✓) if the person has already done the chore, or write an ✗ if the chore isn't done yet. Then decide with your partner who is the best housekeeper. Don't look at your partner's page!

Gina

wash the dishes	✓
sweep the floor	✗
take out the trash	✗
make the bed	✗
feed the cat	✓
iron the clothes	✗

Tony

make the bed	✓
feed the cat	✗
iron the clothes	✗
take out the trash	✓
wash the dishes	✗
sweep the floor	✓

Lynn

iron the clothes	☐
wash the dishes	☐
make the bed	☐
sweep the floor	☐
take out the trash	☐
feed the cat	☐

Pablo

feed the cat	☐
make the bed	☐
sweep the floor	☐
iron the clothes	☐
take out the trash	☐
wash the dishes	☐

The best housekeeper: _____

Useful Language
Has *Lynn or Pablo made her or his bed* yet?
Yes, she or he *has already made* it.
No, she or he *hasn't made* it yet.

Information Gap Activity

Gina, Lynn, Tony, and Pablo are doing their housework. Each has made a list of chores to do. You have the lists for Lynn and Pablo; your partner has the lists for Gina and Tony. Ask each other questions to find out who has finished which chores. In your lists, check (✓) if the person has already done the chore, or write an ✗ if the chore isn't done yet. Then decide with your partner who is the best housekeeper. Don't look at your partner's page!

Gina

- wash the dishes ☐
- sweep the floor ☐
- take out the trash ☐
- make the bed ☐
- feed the cat ☐
- iron the clothes ☐

Tony

- make the bed ☐
- feed the cat ☐
- iron the clothes ☐
- take out the trash ☐
- wash the dishes ☐
- sweep the floor ☐

Lynn

- iron the clothes ☒
- wash the dishes ☑
- make the bed ☑
- sweep the floor ☑
- take out the trash ☒
- feed the cat ☑

Pablo

- feed the cat ☑
- make the bed ☑
- sweep the floor ☑
- iron the clothes ☒
- take out the trash ☑
- wash the dishes ☑

The best housekeeper: _____

Useful Language

Has *Gina* or *Tony* made her or his bed yet?
Yes, she or he *has already made* it.
No, she or he *hasn't made* it yet.

Information Gap Activity

Jim Brennan and Gloria Sosa are both applying for the photojournalist position at *Nature Review Magazine*. The magazine wants someone who has lived in a cold climate and has photographed animals. Other desirable qualifications are some knowledge of Tibet and of Burmese languages, climbing experience, the ability to drive a four-wheel-drive vehicle, and experience in using a two-way radio.

Look at the checklist of Jim's and Gloria's knowledge and skills. You have some of the information; your partner has the rest. To find the missing information, ask your partner questions about each candidate. Write the answers in your book. Then decide who is the best candidate for the job. Don't look at your partner's page!

Name:	Jim Brennan	Gloria Sosa
Nationality:	American	American
Date of Birth:	December 9, 1958	May 24, 1980
College degree:	B.S. Veterinary Science	
Has lived in a cold climate?		Yes
Has photographed animals?	Yes	
Knowledge of Tibet?		Yes
Has been on expeditions?	Yes	
Drives a four-wheel-drive vehicle?		No
Uses a two-way radio?	Yes	
Languages spoken:	English and Burmese	
Sports, Interests:		Photography, mountain climbing

Useful Language

Has Jim Brennan lived in a cold climate?
What languages does Gloria Sosa speak?
I recommend _____ for the position because . . .

Information Gap Activity Student B

Jim Brennan and Gloria Sosa are both applying for the photojournalist position at Nature *Review Magazine*. The magazine wants someone who has lived in a cold climate and has photographed animals. Other desirable qualifications are some knowledge of Tibet and of Burmese languages, climbing experience, the ability to drive a four-wheel-drive vehicle, and experience in using a two-way radio.

Look at the checklist of Jim's and Gloria's knowledge and skills. You have some of the information; your partner has the rest. To find the missing information, ask your partner questions about each candidate. Write the answers in your book. Then decide who is the best candidate for the job.

Name:	Jim Brennan	Gloria Sosa
Nationality:	American	American
Date of Birth:	December 9, 1958	May 24, 1980
College degree:		B.A. Journalism
Has lived in a cold climate?	No	
Has photographed animals?		No
Knowledge of Tibet?	No	
Has been on expeditions?		No
Drives a four-wheel-drive vehicle?	Yes	
Uses a two-way radio?		No
Languages spoken:		English and Spanish
Sports, Interests:	Rock climbing	

Useful Language

Has Jim Brennan been on expeditions?
Can Gloria Sosa drive a four-wheel-drive vehicle?
I recommend _____ for the position because . . .

Look at the chart about the vacation plans of Pablo, Lynn, Jim, Oscar, and Gina. Find out the missing information by asking your partner questions about each person's travel plans. Write the missing information in the chart below. Don't look at your partner's page!

	Pablo	Lynn	JIm	Oscar	Gina
Month of vacation			July		August
Length of vacation	4 days	2 weeks		1 month	
Country to be visited		Spain		China	Japan
Traveling companion	Classmates	Parents		None	
Lodging in country to be visited			Family	Trailer camp	Stay with friends
Activities while there		Tour museums		Shop	

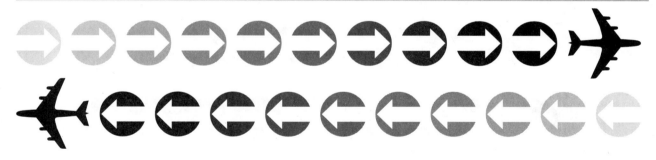

Useful Language

When will *(name)* **visit** _____?
How long will *(name)* **stay there?**
What country will *(name)* **travel to?**
Where will *(name)* **stay in** _____?
Who will *(name)* **travel with?**
What will *(name)* **do in** _____?

Look at the chart about the vacation plans of Pablo, Lynn, Jim, Oscar, and Gina. Find out the missing information by asking your partner questions about each person's travel plans. Write the missing information in the chart below. Don't look at your partner's page!

	Pablo	**Lynn**	**JIm**	**Oscar**	**Gina**
Month of vacation	June	December		September	
Length of vacation			8 weeks		10 days
Country to be visited	Mexico		Italy		
Traveling companion			His wife		None
Lodging in country to be visited	Camp on beach	A four-star hotel			
Activities while there	Sunbathe Surf		Ride in a gondola		Go horseback riding

Useful Language

When will (name) **visit** _____?
How long will (name) **stay there?**
What country will (name) **travel to?**
Where will (name) **stay in** _____?
Who will (name) **travel with?**
What will (name) **do in** _____?